WHY ARE YOU ATHEISTS SO ANGRY?

WHY ARE YOU ATHEISTS SO ANGRY?

——— ✸ ———

99 Things That Piss Off the Godless

GRETA CHRISTINA

PITCHSTONE PUBLISHING
Charlottesville, Virginia

Pitchstone Publishing
Charlottesville, Virginia 22901
www.pitchstonepublishing.com

To contact the publisher, please e-mail info@pitchstonepublishing.com
To contact the author, please e-mail greta@gretachristina.com

Printed in the United States of America

19 18 17 16 15 14 13 12   1 2 3 4 5

Library of Congress Cataloging-in-Publication Data

Christina, Greta.
 Why are you atheists so angry? : 99 things that piss off the godless / Greta Christina.
   p. cm.
 ISBN 978-0-9852815-2-6 (pbk. : alk. paper)
 1. Atheism. 2. Common fallacies. 3. Religion—Controversial literature. I. Title.
 BL2747.3.C475 2012
 211'.8—dc23
                      2012016785

Portions of this book were originally published on Greta Christina's Blog, freethoughtblogs.com/greta, and on AlterNet, alternet.org.

Cover design by Casimir Fornalski, casimirfornalski.com

For Ingrid.

"The supreme task is to organize and unite people so that their anger becomes a transforming force."
— Dr. Martin Luther King, Jr.

"I have learned through bitter experience the one supreme lesson: to conserve my anger, and as heat conserved is transmitted into energy, even so our anger controlled can be transmitted into a power that can move the world."
— Mahatma Gandhi

TABLE OF CONTENTS

INTRODUCTION

"Why are you atheists so angry?"

This is a question on a lot of people's minds these days. In the last few years, the atheist movement has moved into overdrive. It's become more visible, more vocal, more activist, better organized, and much less apologetic. And this increased visibility is putting atheist anger into the spotlight. A lot of non-atheists are baffled and disconcerted—to say the least—at what they see as a sudden torrent of atheist anger from apparently out of nowhere.

But like a lot of atheists, I get tired of hearing believers ask, "Why are you so angry?" To me—and to many atheists, agnostics, humanists, freethinkers, brights, and other godless people—the answer seems obvious.

I wanted to answer this question once and for all... so I wouldn't have to answer it anymore.

So I wrote this book.

I wrote it for other atheists—to give a voice to thoughts and feelings they haven't been able to put into words. I wrote it for religious believers—to give a sincere, thoughtful answer to this question, and to explain this phenomenon of outspoken, often angry atheism that's been exploding in the last few years. And I wrote it for atheists who are constantly getting asked, "Why are you so angry?" by their religious family and friends. I wrote it so they'd have an easy way to answer it. "You want to know why I'm angry? Here—read this book!"

The heart of the book is what I've been calling "The Litany of Rage." It's Chapter One. In it, I spell out—exactly and extensively—why so many atheists are so angry. Be sure to take your blood pressure medication first. If you don't get mad when you read it, you're not paying attention.

I know from experience the kinds of reactions that the Litany of Rage is likely to provoke. "You're not being fair!" "You're lumping all religions together!" "You're just as intolerant as the religious extremists you're angry at!" "All that anger is just hurting your cause!" Etc. In Chapter 2, I look at these questions, and patiently take them apart.

And a lot of people are going to say, "But that's not religion's fault! People do bad things to each other for all sorts of reasons! You can't blame religion for all the terrible things done in its name!" In Chapter 3, I explain why I passionately disagree. Religion is unique—and the things that make religion unique are what make it uniquely capable of causing terrible harm.

A lot of religious believers will read the Litany of Rage, and nod their heads in vigorous agreement. "Yes, that's terrible! It's dreadful to see the horrors committed in God's name!" And then they'll turn right around and say, "But surely you don't mean me!" Moderate and progressive believers; New Age believers; "spiritual but not religious" believers; ecumenical and interfaith believers… when they see atheists' anger about religion, they often think their version is exempt. Or that it should be. So in Chapters 4 through 7, I break the bad news: Yes, this means you. I'm not as angry about your variety of religion as I am about hateful and intolerant religious extremism—but I'm still mad about it. And I'm going to tell you why.

But even if religion does significantly more harm than good—even if the unique nature of religion means it's inherently prone to doing more harm than good—that doesn't mean it's wrong, does it? No, it doesn't. And I care about what is and isn't true. In fact, one of the things that makes me angriest about religion is the way it makes people trivialize reality in favor of their wishful thinking. So in Chapter 8, I explain the Top Ten Reasons I Don't Believe In God. That's not the main question this book is trying to answer—but it's an important question, and it deserves an answer.

And lots of people defend religion by saying that it's useful: it makes people behave better, it gives people comfort, it makes people happy. You know—the way believing in Santa makes little kids behave better and makes them happy. So in Chapter 9, I explain what's wrong with the argument from utility... or, as I call it, "the Santa delusion."

A manifesto isn't much good unless it has a goal, and an action plan. Without that, it's just pointless venting. So in Chapter 10, I talk about what, exactly, I hope to accomplish with my atheist writing and activism—and what I hope the atheist movement is going to accomplish. Chapter 11 defends the very idea of atheist activism—more precisely, the idea of trying to persuade people out of religion. And Chapter 12 points out that resistance is not futile, and that atheist activism can be effective.

You may notice, when you read the Litany of Rage, that much of what makes atheists angry isn't the bad things religious believers do to atheists. A huge amount of our anger is about the bad things believers do to other believers. That's the gist of Chapter 13. Atheists' anger doesn't prove that we're selfish, or joyless, or miserable. It shows that we have compassion, and a sense of justice. We're angry because we see terrible harm all around us, and we feel desperately motivated to stop it.

So now what? Now that you're all riled up about religion—what are you going to do about it? That's how I wind things up. Chapter 14 outlines some broad principles for atheist activism—most importantly, the principle that you should do what you think is fun. And Chapter 15 concludes with an extensive resource guide of organizations, support networks, forums, and places you can go for more information and inspiration.

The book is meant to inform, of course. It's meant to let religious believers—as well as my fellow godless heathens—know about some of the more enraging abuses and injustices caused by religion, or committed in its name. It's meant to answer the question, "Why are you atheists so angry?"—by showing that we have valid reasons for our anger.

But this book is also meant to inspire. I hope other godless people read it and are inspired to take action: to speak out, to join organizations, to start organizations, to take part in atheist communities, to write to their newspapers and their Congresspeople, to become a voting bloc.

And most of all, I hope atheists are inspired to come out of the closet. That's how we combat the stupid stereotypes people have about us. That's how we become a political force to be reckoned with. That's the single most important and effective political action that a godless person can take. If this book inspires anything, I hope it inspires people to tell their friends, their families, their co-workers, everyone, that they are godless.

CHAPTER ONE

—— ✹ ——

Why Are You Atheists So Angry?

I'm an atheist. I'm an angry atheist. And I'm proud to be one. I think angry atheists are right to be angry.

There are serious, deep-rooted problems with the way religion plays out, in the United States and around the world. There are ways that religion plays out—extremely common ways—that lead to abuse, injustice, mistreatment, misery, disempowerment, even violence and death. It makes perfect sense to be angry about them. In fact, when people *aren't* angry about them, I'm baffled.

I'm a happy person most of the time. In fact, I find it hilarious when people hear about this book and tell me, with either concern or contempt, "Boy, you're an angry person. How can you live like that?" I mean, it's not like I'm running around smashing plates and going "Rrrr! Rrrr! Rrrr!" all the time. (I hardly ever do that.)

But far too many people ask, "Why are you atheists so angry?"— without even considering the possibility that we're angry because we have legitimate things to be angry about.

So I want to try to answer this question: "Why are you atheists so angry?" Or rather, since I don't presume to speak for all atheists: Why am I so angry?

• • •

1. I'm angry that according to a recent Gallup poll, 53 percent of Americans would not vote for an atheist for President—even for a qualified candidate from the voters' own party—solely because of their atheism.[1]

2. I'm angry that atheists in the United States are often denied custody of their children, explicitly because of their atheism.[2]

3. I'm angry that it took until 1961 for atheists to be guaranteed the right to serve on juries, testify in court, or hold public office in every state in the country.[3]

4. I'm angry that atheist soldiers—in the U.S. armed forces—have had atheist meetings broken up by Christian superior officers, in direct violation of the First Amendment. I'm angry that evangelical Christian groups are being given exclusive access to proselytize on military bases—again in the U.S. armed forces, again in direct violation of the First Amendment. I'm angry that atheist soldiers who complain about this are being harassed and are even getting death threats, from Christian soldiers and superior officers—yet again, in the U.S. armed forces. And I'm angry that Christians still say smug, sanctimonious things like, "there are no atheists in foxholes." You know why you aren't seeing many atheists in foxholes? Because Christians are threatening to shoot them if they come out.[4]

5. I'm angry at preachers who tell women in their flock to submit to their husbands because it's the will of God, even when their husbands are beating them within an inch of their lives.

6. I'm angry that so many parents and religious leaders terrorize children with vivid, traumatizing stories of eternal burning and torture, to ensure that they'll be too frightened to even question religion. And I'm angry that religious leaders explicitly tell children—and adults, for that matter—that the very questioning of religion and the existence of Hell is a dreadful sin, one that will guarantee that Hell is where they'll end up.

7. I'm angry that children get taught by religion to hate and fear their bodies and their sexuality. And I'm especially angry that female children get taught by religion to hate and fear their femaleness, and that queer children get taught by religion to hate and fear their queerness.

8. I'm angry about the girl from the Muslim family in Delaware who was told—by her public-school, taxpayer-paid teacher—that the red stripes on Christmas candy canes represented Christ's blood, that she had to believe in and be saved by Jesus Christ or she'd be condemned to Hell, and that if she didn't, there was no place for her in his classroom.[5]

9. I'm angry at priests who rape children and tell them it's God's will. No, angry isn't a strong enough word. I am enraged. I am revolted. I am trembling with fury at the very thought of it.

10. And I'm enraged that the Catholic Church consciously, deliberately, repeatedly, for years, acted to protect priests who raped children, and deliberately acted to keep it a secret, placing the Church's reputation as a higher priority than, for fuck's sake, children not being raped. I'm enraged that they shuttled child-raping priests from town to town, failed to inform law enforcement officers and in many cases flat-out stonewalled them, deliberately dumped the child rapists in remote, impoverished villages… and then, when the horror finally came to light, responded with defensive entrenchment, and equated the accusations with either anti-Semitic bigotry or petty gossip. And I'm enraged that the Church actually argued, in court, that protecting child-molesting priests from prosecution, and shuffling those priests from diocese to diocese so they could molest kids in a whole new community that didn't yet suspect them, was a Constitutionally protected form of free religious expression, and that the Church should therefore be immune from prosecution for it.[6]

11. And I'm angry that so many Catholics are so willing to defend the Catholic Church's behavior in the child rape scandal. I'm angry that they're letting their fear of eternal punishment in Hell, their desire

for eternal reward in Heaven, or simply the comfort they take from the soothing rituals and traditions of the Church, take priority over taking the most obvious moral position a person could take—namely, that people and institutions should not protect child rapists. I'm angry that if their softball league, their charity group, their children's school, did what the Catholic Church did and continues to do, they'd almost certainly quit in outrage... but because it's their church, they stay in it, and defend the blatantly indefensible.

12. I'm angry about 9/11.

13. And I'm angry that, after 9/11 happened, people of Middle Eastern descent were attacked and their businesses vandalized, because they were Muslims, or because people assumed they were Muslims even if they weren't, and they blamed all Muslims for the attacks.

14. And I'm angry that Jerry Falwell blamed 9/11 on pagans, abortionists, feminists, gays and lesbians, the ACLU, and the People For the American Way. I'm angry that this theology of a wrathful god exacting revenge against pagans and abortionists by sending radical Muslims to blow up a building full of secretaries and investment bankers... this was not some fringe theology held by a handful of weirdos picketing funerals. This was a theology held by a powerful, wealthy, widely-respected religious leader with millions of followers.[7]

15. I'm angry that the Bamiyan Buddha statues in Afghanistan—magnificent, monumental works of art over fifteen hundred years old—were dynamited by the Taliban, because they were idols, and were believed to be an affront to God's law.[8]

16. I'm angry about circumcision. I'm angry that, in the United States in the 21st century, millions of people are still cutting off part of their sons' genitals, for no good medical reason and against all good medical advice, because Bronze-age goat-herders thousands of years ago thought their god demanded it.

17. I'm angry that little girls are getting their clitorises cut off because their parents' religion teaches that it's necessary.

18. And I'm angry that so many people defend religion against the charge of female genital mutilation by saying, "Oh, but that's not what the religion really teaches, if you look at the original text, blah blah blah…" The fact is that the Islamic religion as it is widely believed and practiced—as well as other religions as they are widely believed and practiced (this practice is not limited to Islam)—teaches that little girls need to have their clitorises cut off… and it enrages me that so many people react to this fact by defending the religion and not the children.

19. I'm angry about the Protocols of the Elders of Zion. I'm angry that a forged document claiming to be a Jewish plot for global domination—not just a fraud, but a pathetically obvious fraud—was taken seriously and widely disseminated as fact. I'm angry that this forgery was used for decades, by individuals and governments, from Russia to Nazi Germany to Egypt to the United States, to justify hatred and fear of Jews… even to the point of justifying their systematic extermination. I'm angry that this continued to happen for decades after the document was conclusively shown to be a fraud, and that it continues to be taken seriously by many to this day.[9]

20. I'm angry about honor killings. I'm angry that in Islamic theocracies, women who have sex outside marriage, women who date outside their religion, women who spend time with male friends, women who disobey their male relatives, are routinely executed. I'm angry that in these theocracies, even women who have been raped get executed for the crime of adultery. I'm angry that the ones who are only beaten and imprisoned are the ones who get off lucky.

21. I'm angry that, in Islamic theocracies, girls as young as nine years old can be married against their will.

22. I'm angry that, when a nine-year-old girl in Brazil was raped, the doctors who performed an abortion on her, and her family who approved the abortion, were excommunicated by the Catholic Church. And I'm angry that there was no excommunication for her stepfather who raped her.[10]

23. I'm angry that seriously ill children needlessly suffer and die because their parents believe in faith healing or believe that medical treatment will anger their god. And I'm angry that, in thirty-nine states in the United States, these parents are protected from prosecution for child neglect.[11]

24. I'm angry that, in fourteen states in the United States, child care centers operated by religious organizations don't have to adhere to basic standards of health and safety, and don't even have to be licensed. I'm angry that children in these child care centers have been harmed and have even died because of poor or non-existent staff training or grossly unsafe conditions, and that the operators are immune from prosecution.[12]

25. I'm angry at the Sunday school teacher who told comic artist Craig Thompson that he couldn't draw in Heaven. And I'm angry that she said it with the complete conviction of authority… when she had no basis whatsoever for that assertion. How the hell did she know what Heaven was like? How could she possibly know that you could sing in Heaven but not draw? And why on Earth would you say something that squelching and dismissive to a talented child?

26. I'm angry that almost half of Americans believe in creationism. Not a broad, theistic evolution, "God had a hand in evolution" version of creationism, but a strict, young-Earth, "God created man in his present form at one time within the last 10,000 years" creationism.[13]

I should clarify this one, as people often misunderstand it. When atheists say that we're angry about how many creationists there are in the U.S., a common response is, "What business is that of yours? Don't they have the right to believe whatever they want? You're just as intolerant of their beliefs as they are of yours!"

So let me explain. If creationists are trying to get their religious beliefs taught in the public schools—paid for by everyone's taxes, forced on children whose families don't share those beliefs, in direct violation of the First Amendment—then it isn't just their own business, and I have a right to be angry about it.

But if they're not trying to do any of that—if they're just ordinary people trying to get by, working two jobs to pay the bills, and they're leaving their school boards alone—then I'm not angry at them.

I'm angry for them.

I'm angry that they've been taught to fear and scorn one of the most profound, powerful truths about the world, and to embrace a lie that flatly contradicts an overwhelming body of evidence. I'm angry that they've been taught that loving their god means rejecting the reality of the Universe he supposedly created. I'm angry that they've been taught that scientists—people who care so much about the Universe they devote their lives to painstakingly figuring out how it works—are wicked and evil. I'm angry that they've been taught that virtuous religious faith demands that they disconnect themselves from the march of human knowledge.

I'm not angry at them. I'm angry on their behalf.

27. On this topic: I'm angry that school boards across the United States are still—more than eight decades after the Scopes trial—having to spend time and money and resources on the fight to have evolution taught in the schools. School boards are not exactly loaded with time and money and resources, and when they spend it fighting this stupid fight, they're not spending it, you know, teaching.[14]

28. And, in a similar vein: I'm angry that science teachers in the U.S. public schools often don't teach evolution, or give it only a cursory mention, even when teaching it is sanctioned and indeed required—because they're afraid of sparking controversy and having to deal with angry fundamentalist parents. Evolution is the foundation of the science of biology—biology literally doesn't make sense without it—and kids who aren't being taught about evolution are being deprived of one of the most fundamental ways we have of understanding ourselves and the world.

29. I'm angry that right-wing Christians in the United States are actively campaigning against anti-bullying laws in elementary and high schools, on the grounds that religious freedom includes the right to harass, threaten, and intimidate gay kids.[15]

30. I'm angry that, in public, taxpayer-paid high schools around the country, atheist students who are trying to organize clubs—something they're legally allowed to do—are routinely getting stonewalled by school administrators. I'm angry that the Secular Student Alliance has to push high school administrators on a regular basis, and in some cases they've even had to be sued, simply to get them to obey the law.[16]

31. I'm angry about what happened to Jessica Ahlquist. I'm angry that, in a public, taxpayer-paid high school in Rhode Island, a banner with an official school prayer was prominently posted in the school auditorium—in direct violation of the Constitution and of clear, well-established legal precedent. I'm angry that when Ahlquist asked her high school to take down the banner, her request was rejected, and she had to go to court to get her school to comply with the law. And I'm angry that, when she won her lawsuit—in an entirely unsurprising, non-controversial ruling—she was targeted with a barrage of brutal threats, including threats of beating, rape, and death.[17]

32. I'm angry about what happened to Damon Fowler. I'm angry that when he asked his public, taxpayer-paid high school to stop a school-sponsored prayer at his graduation, he was hounded, pilloried, and ostracized by his community, publicly demeaned by one of his own teachers, targeted with threats of violence and death, and kicked out of his house by his parents.[18]

33. And I'm angry that what happened to Jessica Ahlquist and Damon Fowler are not isolated incidents. I'm angry that things like this are happening around the United States, and all around the world. I'm angry that, even when the law clearly states that the government can't endorse religion or force it on its citizens, people are often too intimidated to insist on their legal rights... because they're afraid they'll

be bullied, ostracized, and threatened with violence by their classmates, their co-workers, their communities, their friends, even their families. I'm angry that this doesn't just happen to atheists: It happens to Jews, Muslims, Buddhists, Wiccans, religious minorities of all varieties. And I'm angry because these people aren't wrong to be afraid.

34. And I'm angry that people hear stories like this… and still insist that atheists don't suffer from discrimination and should stop complaining about it, because we have protection under the law. I get angry when people blithely ignore the fact that legal protection doesn't do much good if people are intimidated out of demanding it.

35. I'm angry that, when my dad had a stroke and went into a nursing home, the staff asked my brother, "Is he Baptist or Catholic?" And I'm not just angry on behalf of my atheist dad. I'm angry on behalf of all the Jews, all the Buddhists, all the Muslims, all the neo-Pagans, whose families almost certainly got asked that same question. Heck— I'm angry on behalf of the Lutherans and Methodists and Presbyterians whose families got asked that question. That question is enormously disrespectful, not just of my dad's atheism, but of everyone at that nursing home who wasn't Baptist or Catholic.

36. I'm angry about my wife Ingrid's grandparents. I'm angry that their religious fundamentalism was such a huge source of strife and unhappiness among their family, and that it alienated them from their children and grandchildren. I'm angry that they persistently pressed their religion on Ingrid, to the point that she's still traumatized by it. And I'm angry that their religion, which if nothing else should have been a comfort to them in their old age, was instead a source of anguish and despair—because they knew their children and grandchildren were going to be burned and tortured forever in Hell, and how could Heaven be Heaven if their children and grandchildren were being burned and tortured in Hell?

37. I'm angry that, because of religious bigotry against LGBT people, Ingrid and I had to get married three times, before we finally got

to have a wedding that was legal in our home state. I'm angry that, nine months after our marriage, Catholics and Mormons spent millions of dollars and thousands of hours to pass Prop 8 and make it impossible for any other same-sex couples in California to marry. I'm angry that our marriage is still not seen as a real marriage in (as of this writing) 42 of the 50 states.[19] I'm angry that, when we travel to places like Missouri or Colorado, we have to worry about what happens if one of us has to go to the hospital—will the other be able to make decisions on our behalf, or even be able to visit? I'm angry that even our federal government won't recognize our marriage as real—because fear of offending the religious right controls how laws get made in this country. And I'm angry that religious and political leaders are scoring points by exploiting fears about sexuality in a changing world, fanning the flames of those fears… and giving people a religious excuse for why their fears are justified.

38. I'm angry about "lying for the Lord."[20] I'm angry that the Mormon Church officially advocates a policy of deception, concealment, exaggeration, selective disclosure, censorship, and outright dishonesty about the history and tenets of their religion—aimed at both the general public and members of their own church—in order to protect their image. I'm angry that Mormons who have violated this policy, and who told the truth about the church's history and teachings even when it was unflattering, have been excommunicated.

39. I'm angry about Mormons baptizing people into the Mormon Church after they're dead. I'm angry that thousands of Jewish Holocaust victims were posthumously baptized into the Mormon faith. I'm angry that Mitt Romney's family baptized his father-in-law—Edward Roderick Davies, a staunch atheist who referred to religion as "drudgery" and "hogwash"—after his death.[21]

I know. This one seems weird. If I'm an atheist, and I don't believe in any sort of afterlife… why should it matter what happens to dead people? Once you're gone and are rotting in the ground, what difference does it make whether someone writes your name on a piece of paper and dunks it into a tub of magic water?

It matters because freedom of conscience matters.

It matters because one of the central pillars of human rights is the right to come to our own conclusions about religion. We have the right to go to our deathbed with our own judgments about God and the afterlife. If there is nothing else in the world that is entirely our own, we still have the insides of our heads. And having someone else come along after we die, dunk our names in a tub of magic water, and say, "You thought you were an atheist or a Catholic or a Jew—but guess what! You're a Mormon!"… that is profoundly screwed-up.

If the Mormon theology were right, and only people who've been dunked in the tub of magic water (alive or dead) could enter the glorious afterlife… that is one messed-up theology. And if it's wrong—as I obviously think it is—then it's degrading, invasive, and disrespectful of people's most basic rights: the right to go to our grave with our own conscience, our own free will, and our own decisions and conclusions about some of the most important questions that human beings face.

40. I'm angry that, in fundamentalist Mormon polygamous cults, girls are raised from birth to believe that they'll be tormented for eternity in the afterlife if they don't marry whatever man they're ordered to by their preacher. In most cases when they're teenagers. In many cases as young as thirteen. In some cases, younger.[22] And I'm angry that, in these same cults, teenage boys are routinely terrorized, kicked out of the community, and exiled from their families, on the flimsiest of pretenses, just so there's less competition for marriageable girls.[23]

41. And I'm angry that, in the non-fundamentalist, non-polygamous, entirely mainstream Mormon church, girls are raised from birth to believe that they'll be tormented for eternity in the afterlife if they don't marry, bear lots of children, and be submissive to their husbands… and gay kids are raised from birth to believe that they'll be

tormented for eternity in the afterlife if they don't suppress and deny their sexuality.

42. And on a related topic: I'm angry that, in Salt Lake City, Utah, 40 percent of all homeless teenagers are gay[24]—most of them kids who have been kicked out of their homes by their Mormon families.

43. I'm angry about the lesbian veteran who came to her VA hospital seeking help for depression… and who left the hospital three hours later determined to kill herself, because a Marine Corps nurse harangued her for three hours about her "lifestyle of sin" and whether she'd been "saved by Jesus Christ."[25] I'm angry that any health care professional in the world would place their religious proselytizing as a higher priority than the immediate health crisis of a patient in their care. And I'm especially angry that this religious harassment took place at a United States government institution, by a government employee acting as a representative of the country.

44. I'm angry that in Jerusalem, because of pressure from ultra-Orthodox Jewish leaders, a major conference on gynecology refused to allow any women to speak.[26] And I'm angry that this didn't happen in the 15th century, or the 19th: it happened this year, 2012, the year this book is being published.

45. I'm angry about "modesty patrols." I'm angry that in Jerusalem, women and girls who don't adhere to the modesty standards of ultra-Orthodox Jewish leaders are harassed, terrorized, spat on, and physically assaulted. I'm angry that girls who appear in public with boys have been pepper-sprayed; that women who wear red blouses have had rocks thrown at them; that a woman who didn't obey a fellow passenger's order to move to the back of the bus was beaten; that stores selling clothes regarded as provocative have been vandalized; that stores selling MP4 players that could possibly be used to view pornography have been torched.[27] I'm angry that even an eight-year-old girl, Naama Margolese, was subjected to a mob who screamed at her, spat on her, and called her a whore, for walking to school with her arms exposed.[28]

46. I'm angry that the Hasidic newspaper *Di Tzitung* erased U.S. Secretary of State Hillary Clinton from an important and historic group photograph, because their religious beliefs hold that publishing photographs of women is immodest and could be sexually suggestive. And I'm angry that their supposed "apology" for this action insisted that their policy of never publishing photographs of women, and thus expunging them from the historical record, "in no way relegates them to a lower status."[29]

47. I'm angry about Israel and Palestine.

48. I'm angry about the Holocaust.

49. And I'm angry that people try to blame the Holocaust on atheists and atheism. No, Hitler was not an atheist. That's a myth. All the best evidence overwhelmingly confirms that Hitler had religious beliefs. And religion was one of the central justifications for the Nazi Party's persecution of the Jews, and for the calculated extermination of six million of them.[30]

50. I'm angry that people in Africa—including children—are being terrorized, driven from their homes, tortured, maimed, and killed, over accusations of witchcraft. Not in the Middle Ages; not in the 1600s. Now. Today.[31]

51. I'm angry that the belief in karma and reincarnation gets used as a justification for the caste system in India. I'm angry that people born into poverty and despair are taught that it's their fault, that they must have done something bad in a previous life, and the misery they were born into is their punishment for it.

52. I'm angry about what happened to Galileo. Still. I realize that it happened in 1633: I'm still mad. And I'm angry that it took the Catholic Church until 1992 to apologize for it.

For those of you who don't know what happened to Galileo: For the crime of publishing a book showing that the Earth went around the Sun, he was ordered to recant, had his book and any future books he might publish banned, and was sentenced to house arrest for the rest of his life... because the theory that the Earth went around the Sun contradicted Holy Scripture.

53. And I'm angry that what happened to Galileo was, relatively speaking, a walk in the park. I'm angry that astronomer Giordano Bruno was burned at the stake for (among other things) advocating the position that the Sun was simply one star among many. Let me spell that one out: For advocating scientific positions that were contrary to Church doctrine, the man was tied to a stake in a public square, set fire to, and burned to death.

54. I'm angry on behalf of the atheist blogger in Iran who told me they have to blog anonymously because if they're discovered, they'll be executed.

55. I'm angry that people are dying of AIDS in Africa, because the Catholic Church convinced them that using condoms makes Baby Jesus cry.[32]

56. I'm angry that women are having dangerous and even deadly illegal abortions—or are being forced to have unwanted children who in many cases they resent and mistreat—because religious organizations have gotten laws passed making abortion illegal or inaccessible.

57. And I'm angry that abortion rates go up when schools teach the deceptive, hysterical, flatly untrue version of sex education known as "abstinence-only"[33]... and that religious opponents of abortion still advocate abstinence-only sex ed, and still oppose giving teenagers access to birth control and accurate, evidence-based information about sex. I'm angry that, even though these believers claim to care about abortion because they care about the life of undeveloped embryos, they actually place a higher priority on their real agenda: enforcing the sexual morality of their religion.

58. I get angry when religious leaders opportunistically use religion, and people's trust and faith in religion, to steal, cheat, lie, manipulate the political process, take sexual advantage of their followers, and generally behave like the scum of the earth. I get angry when it

happens over and over and over again. I get angry that when we see a newspaper headline reading "Religious Leader Steals, Cheats, Lies, Manipulates Political Process, Takes Sexual Advantage of Followers, Generally Behaves Like Scum of Earth," we shrug and think, "Oh, yeah, must be Tuesday. So what else is new?" And I get angry when people see this happening, and still say that atheism is bad—because without religion, people would have no basis for morality or ethics, and no reason not to just do whatever they wanted.

59. I get angry when religious believers make arguments against atheism—and make accusations against atheists—without having bothered to talk to any atheists, or read any atheist writing, or freaking well spend ten minutes Googling the word "atheism" to find out what we actually think and say. I get angry when they trot out the same old crap about how "atheism is a nihilistic philosophy, with no joy or meaning to life and no basis for morality or ethics"... when if they spent ten minutes in the atheist blogosphere, they would discover countless atheists who experience great joy and meaning in our lives, and are intensely concerned about right and wrong. I realize that ten minutes of Googling is a dreadful inconvenience... but if you're going to be bigoted and hateful against millions of people, it seems like the least you could do.

60. I get angry when believers glorify religious faith—i.e., believing in a supernatural world with no good evidence supporting that belief—as a positive virtue, a character trait that makes people good and noble. I get angry when they base their entire philosophy of life on what is, at best, a hunch; when they ignore or reject or rationalize any evidence that contradicts that hunch or calls it into question. And I get angry when they do this... and then accuse atheists of being close-minded and ignoring the truth.

61. I get angry when believers say they can know the truth—the greatest truth of all about the nature of the Universe, namely the source of all existence—simply by sitting quietly and listening to their

hearts… and then accuse atheists of being arrogant. And this attitude isn't just arrogant towards atheists. It's arrogant towards people of other religions who have sat just as quietly, listened to their hearts with just as much sincerity, and come to completely opposite conclusions about God and the soul and the Universe.

62. And I get angry when believers say that the entire unimaginable hugeness of the Universe was made specifically for the human race—when atheists, by contrast, say that humanity is a microscopic dot on a microscopic dot, an infinitesimal eyeblink in the vastness of time and space—and then, once again, believers accuse atheists of being arrogant.

I want to take a moment and explain why I get so angry about believers making bad arguments for religion, and why I'm spending a chunk of time raging about it. I mean, compared to burned witches and raped children and homeless gay teenagers, "atheists being annoyed on the Internet" is hardly the crime of the century.

But it still makes me angry. I get angry because they're not arguing in good faith. I get angry because they're refusing to see their privilege. I get angry because so many of these bad arguments for religion end up perpetuating misinformation and bigotry against atheists. I get angry because they're wasting our time. And I get angry because they're prioritizing their wishful thinking over reality—and I care passionately about reality, and get ticked off when people treat it like a petty nuisance.

63. I'm angry that I have to know more about their damn religion than they do. I get angry when believers say things about the tenets and texts of their own religion that are flatly untrue, and I have to correct them on it.

64. I get angry when believers treat any criticism of their religion—i.e., pointing out that their religion is a hypothesis about the world, and asking it to stand on its own in the marketplace of ideas—as insulting and intolerant. I get angry when believers accuse atheists of

being intolerant for saying things like, "I don't agree with you," "I think you're mistaken about that," and "What evidence do you have to support that?"

65. I'm angry that Christians in the United States—members of the single most powerful and influential religious group in the country, in the wealthiest and most powerful country in the world—act like beleaguered victims, martyrs being thrown to the lions all over again, whenever anyone criticizes them or they don't get their way.

66. And I get angry when Christians in the United States—especially the Christian Right—try to have it both ways on the "persecuted martyr/favored majority" question. I get angry when they play the "Christian nation" card, saying "majority rules, there are more of us then there are of you, we get to push the rest of you around and make everyone play the way we want"... and then, when it's politically expedient, they turn around and howl about how Christians are being persecuted by the secular humanist power structure, and how Christianity is in grave danger of being eradicated. Those things can't both be true. Pick one.

67. I'm angry that huge swaths of public policy in this country—about same-sex marriage, birth control, abortion, stem-cell research, physician-assisted suicide, sex education in schools—are being based, not on evidence of which policies do and don't work and what is and isn't true about the world, but on religious texts written hundreds or thousands of years ago, and on believers' personal feelings about how those texts should be interpreted, with no supporting evidence whatsoever... and no apparent concept of why any evidence should be needed.

68. I'm angry that when people run for political office in the United States, it's considered legitimate to grill them about their employment background, their positions on legislation, their positions on social issues, the taxes they've paid, even their sexual history... but it's considered invasive and intolerant to ask if they believe in talking snakes, demonic possession, magic underwear, magic crackers that turn

into the flesh of their god, an Earth that was created 6,000 years ago, or a god who put himself on Earth in human form and then sacrificed himself to himself to atone for sins that other people committed and to save humanity from the punishment he himself was planning to dole out. If someone is going to make decisions about science funding, emerging medical technology, our educational system, and so on... I think it matters if they believe any of that shit, and I bloody well want to know about it.

69. I'm angry about the industrial schools operated by the Catholic Church in Ireland. I'm angry that children incarcerated in these "schools" were subjected to starvation, neglect, beatings, sexual abuse, and physical abuse that can only be described as torture, in some cases resulting in death. I'm angry that this went on for decades. And I'm angry that, for decades, multiple reports of these abuses were ignored, dismissed, and even actively suppressed by the Irish government... not just because of the immense political power of the Catholic Church in Ireland, but because of the preposterous level of deference the Church was held in.[34]

70. I'm angry about the Magdalene laundries operated by the Catholic Church in Ireland. I'm angry that for decades—indeed, for well over a century—women who were considered sexually immoral, including unwed mothers, prostitutes, sexually active teenagers, women who had left their husbands, disobedient servants, overly flirtatious girls, and more—were imprisoned and held against their will in what amounted to forced labor camps. I'm angry that they were physically abused, psychologically abused, forcibly separated from their children, and forced into endless days of backbreaking labor to profit the Church, in many cases for the rest of their lives. I'm angry that they would have been better off in prison: that they were held on the sole authority of the Church, with no legal recourse, no due process, and no possibility of appeal. And I'm angry that all this was done in the name of enforcing a divine code of goodness and morality.[35]

71. I'm angry about exorcism.[36] I'm angry that, for centuries, people with mental and physical illness were subjected to mental and physical torture in order to drive out non-existent demons. And I'm angry that this isn't a relic of the Middle Ages. I'm angry that now, today, in the 21st century, people are being subjected to torture—actual, literal torture—because of the archaic, patently ridiculous belief in demonic possession. I'm angry that you can actually watch these exorcisms on television—and there isn't a massive public outcry against it.[37]

72. I'm angry that religion was used as a rationalization for slavery. I'm angry that slave-owners in the United States were taught that God intended them to own other human beings as property... and religious leaders cited the Bible to support this practice. I'm angry that slaves in the United States were taught that being owned as property by other human beings was God's will, and that it was their duty to God to submit to their masters.... and, again, this practice was supported with text from the Bible. And I'm angry that there is, in fact, Biblical doctrine supporting the practice of slavery.

73. And I'm angry that people look at the history of slavery in the United States, and at the religious rationalizations given for it... and still insist that religion and the Bible provide the moral foundation for our culture. I'm angry that people can look at a holy book that firmly prohibits eating shellfish, wearing blended fabrics, planting two kinds of crops in the same field—and yet says not one word prohibiting the ownership of other human beings as property, and in fact says many positive things supporting the practice—and will still insist that this book is the primary source for the morality of our society.

74. And I'm angry about the revisionist history that gets done about religion and slavery. I'm angry at how Christians today proudly claim that religion is what inspired the abolitionists... while they conveniently dismiss the overwhelming support given by the churches to

the institution of slavery, and ignore the fervent opposition to slavery from so many atheists, freethinkers, and opponents of organized religion.

75. I'm angry about Salman Rushdie.[38] I'm angry that, because he wrote a novel with some ideas that some fundamentalist religious leaders found upsetting, he was targeted, not with passionate disagreement, not with social disapproval, not even with an Islamic version of excommunication, but with hit men. I'm angry that he had to go into hiding, for years, because he was being pursued by fanatical thugs who were trying to murder him. I'm angry that bookstores carrying this book were firebombed; that several people involved in publishing the book were violently attacked; that the book's Japanese translator, Hitoshi Igarashi, was murdered; and that in a mob's attempt to murder another of the book's translators, thirty-five people were killed.[39]

76. I'm angry about Ayaan Hirsi Ali. I'm angry that, when she was a child, her clitoris was cut off. I'm angry that her family tried to force her into an unwanted marriage to a man she despised. And I'm angry that, because she had the temerity to speak out against these abuses, and against the religion that endorsed and supported them, she has been targeted with hit men, and has to live with heightened security and in fear of her life.[40]

77. I'm angry about Theo Van Gogh. I'm angry that, because he made a film with some ideas that some fundamentalist religious leaders found upsetting, he was, in fact, murdered.[41]

78. I'm angry about Quiverfull families. I'm angry that women are pressured by their religion into having as many babies as their bodies will produce—even if they don't want them, even if they can't take care of them, even if it chains them to abusive husbands, even if it makes it impossible to care for the children they already have, even if it destroys their physical and mental health. I'm angry that these women are taught that the only life God wants for them is a life of obeying men and creating an army of Christian children to overtake the world.[42]

79. I'm angry that, in the Church of Scientology, members are reportedly pressured to cut themselves off from friends or family members who criticize Scientology. I'm angry that, according to reports, students in Scientology schools have been reported for ethics violations simply for researching opposition to Scientology. I'm angry that leaders in the Church are reportedly violently abusive to their members—and that victims of abuse within the church are reportedly punished if they seek outside help. I'm angry that children brought up in Scientology—particularly in the Sea Org, an internal order within the church—are reportedly exploited, physically abused, denied medical care, forced into abusive labor conditions, and are denied formal education and kept isolated from the outside world, making it almost impossible for them to function in the outside world if they do manage to escape. And I'm angry that, when I write about Scientology, I keep having to say "reportedly"—because even though these incidents are very well-documented and have been widely discussed and reported on, the church is notoriously litigious. (Reportedly.)[43]

80. I'm angry that, in many Buddhist monasteries, children as young as ten years old are inducted as novice monks. I'm angry that children who can't possibly understand the tenets and demands of the religion are recruited into devoting their lives to it. And I'm especially angry because the children who become novice monks are typically among the most impoverished—and they're drawn into abandoning secular life and devoting their lives to the monastery, not out of a sincere religious calling, but out of a need for food and shelter.[44]

81. I'm angry that the current Dalai Lama said that sex can only provide short-term pleasure and is inherently destructive in the long term, even leading to suicide and murder[45]; that all forms of sexuality other than penis-in-vagina intercourse are banned by Buddhist teachings[46]; and that, although he supports the tolerance of gay people, he sees homosexual sex as "wrong," "unwholesome," a "bad action,"

"vices," "not acceptable from a Buddhist point of view," and "contrary to Buddhist ethics."[47]

82. I'm angry that, in Sri Lanka, the Buddhist majority has perpetrated intimidation, vandalism, and violence against Christians and Christian churches.[48]

83. And I'm angry that, when criticisms of religion are leveled, Buddhism all too often gets a free pass. I'm angry that the Westernized version of Buddhism typically ignores or dismisses these abuses. I'm angry that the versions of Buddhism practiced in Nepal or Thailand or Sri Lanka get treated as marginal or trivial, while the version of Buddhism practiced in California is somehow seen as the true faith.

84. I'm angry that, when atheists criticize right-wing religious extremism, progressive believers say "But we're not all like that! What about progressive religion?"… but when we criticize progressive religion, progressive believers get hurt, and say, "But we're on your side! Why are you alienating your allies?"

85. I get angry when believers say at the beginning of an argument that their belief is based on reason and evidence, and at the end of the argument say things like, "It just seems that way to me," or, "I feel it in my heart." As if that were a clincher. I mean, couldn't they have said that at the beginning of the argument, and not wasted my time? I have better things to do than debate people who pretend to care about evidence and reason but actually don't. I could be playing with our kittens and watching Project Runway.

86. I get angry when believers unhesitatingly attribute every good thing in the world to God—and then respond to bad things by saying, "God works in mysterious ways." If God's ways are so mysterious, and we can't begin to understand his thinking behind tsunamis and drought and pediatric cancer, then what makes you think you understand his intentions when it comes to pretty sunsets or cute puppies or helping you find the peanut butter?

87. I get angry when believers unhesitatingly attribute every good thing in the world to God—and then respond to bad things by saying, "God had to do it that way, his hands were tied." You're telling me that God is powerful and smart enough to create pretty sunsets and help you find the peanut butter, but he's not powerful or smart enough to create a world without tsunamis and drought and pediatric cancer?

88. I'm angry at the unbelievable self-centered pettiness of so much prayer. I get angry when people ask God to help them find the peanut butter... and neglect to ask him to end tsunamis and drought and pediatric cancer.

89. I'm angry that so many religious believers feel guilty or ashamed when someone they love dies, because their religion isn't giving them comfort even though they think it should. I'm angry that, when religion fails on one of its most basic promises—the promise to provide solace in the face of grief—so many believers react by thinking, not that there's something wrong with their religion, but that there's something wrong with them.

90. I get angry when advice columnists tell their troubled letter-writers to talk to their priest or minister or rabbi... when there is no legal requirement that a religious leader have any sort of training in counseling or therapy.

91. And I get angry when religious leaders offer counseling and advice to troubled people—sex advice, relationship advice, advice on depression and stress, etc.—not based on any evidence about what does and doesn't work in people's brains and lives, but on the basis of what their religious doctrine tells them God wants for us.

92. I'm angry about the trustee at a local Presbyterian church who told his teenage daughter that he didn't believe in God or religion, but that it was important to keep up his work because without religion there would be no morality in the world. I'm angry that he, himself, felt capable of accepting a world without God—but thought the

parishioners were too stupid, too weak, or too immoral to do the same, and decided on their behalf that they had to be lied to.

93. I'm angry that the idea of religious faith—the idea that it's acceptable, and even virtuous, to believe things you have no good reason to think are true—leads people to ignore, dismiss, trivialize, and flatly reject reality. I get angry when believers make arguments for religion that amount to—and sometimes flatly state—that they don't care whether the things they believe are true. And I'm not just angry because ignoring and rejecting reality leads people to make bad decisions that hurt themselves and others. I'm angry because reality is freaking awesome—terrible sometimes, for sure, but also delightful and wondrous and more surprising than anything we could make up about it—and it upsets me that so many people shut it out just so they can keep believing their made-up stories.

94. I get angry when believers respond to some or all of these offenses by saying, "Well, that's not the true faith. Hating queers/rejecting science/stifling questions and dissent... that's not the true faith. People who do that aren't real Christians/Jews/Muslims/Hindus/etc." As if they had a pipeline to God. As if they had any reason at all to think that they know for sure what God wants, and that the billions of others who disagree with them obviously have it wrong. (Besides... I'm an atheist. The argument that "Those other guys just aren't doing it right" is not going to cut it with me. I don't think any of you have it right. To me, it all looks like stuff that people made up.)

95. And on that topic: I get angry when religious believers insist that their interpretation of their religion and religious text is the right one, and that fellow believers with an opposite interpretation clearly have it wrong. I get angry when believers insist that the parts about Jesus' prompt return and all prayers being answered are obviously not meant literally... but the parts about Hell and damnation and gay sex being an abomination, that's real. And I get angry when believers insist that the parts about Hell and damnation and gay sex being an

abomination obviously aren't meant literally, but the parts about caring for the poor are actually what God meant. How the hell do they know which parts of the Bible/Torah/Koran/Bhagavad-Gita/whatever are the ones God really meant, and which parts aren't? And if they don't know, if they're just basing it on their own moral instincts and their own perceptions of the world, then on what basis do they think that God and their sacred texts have anything to do with it at all? What reason do they have for acting as if their opinion is the same as God's, and he's totally backing them up on it?

96. And I get angry when believers act as if these offenses aren't important, because "Not all believers act like that. I'm a believer, and I don't act like that." As if that matters. This stuff is a major way that religion plays out in our world, and it makes me furious to hear religious believers minimize it because it's not how it happens to play out for them.

97. I'm angry that, when I wrote the piece on my blog about atheist anger, I got comments telling me, quote, "It's a pity your mother didn't have an abortion." "I hope some guys bomb your house bitch." "Just kill yourself, k?" "What you need is to get laid. Not with lesbian toys either. You need a strong man with some big junk and a strong will to set you straight." "I fucking hate every single person who posted here, and if there were some magical button that I could press which could annihilate your collective existence in an instant, I would push it 1728 times." "You're a fat, ugly whore. Your anger doesn't impress me. Go drink bleach."[49] I'm angry that writing my atheist opinions—angry opinions, yes, but opinions where I was careful to distinguish between criticizing behaviors and insulting people, on a blog that people are free to read or not as they like—resulted in me fearing for my safety and my life.

98. And of course, I get angry—sputteringly, inarticulately, pulse-racingly angry—when believers chide atheists for being so angry. "Why do you have to be so angry all the time?" "All that anger is so

off-putting." "If atheism is so great, then why are so many of you so angry?"

I look at all the horrors I wrote about in this book. I look at mutilated children. I look at demolished art. I look at people suffering and dying because of faith healing. I look at organized Christianity—not just the religious right, but supposedly "moderate" churches as well—interfering with AIDS prevention, getting their theology in the public schools, trying to stop me and Ingrid from getting married, protecting priests who rape children. I look at fatwas, and burqas, and 9/11, and Salman Rushdie having to go into hiding for years. I look at the caste system in India, and the religious justifications that get used to defend it. I look at girl children in Jerusalem being spat on by a mob for baring their arms.

And I look at atheists occasionally being mean-spirited and snarky in blogs and books and magazines.

And I think: Can we please have some perspective?

Do you seriously look at all of this crap I'm talking about, thousands of years of abuse and injustice, deceit and willful ignorance, brutality and exploitation—and then look at a few years of atheists being snarky on the Internet—and see them as somehow equivalent?

Or worse: Do you somehow see the snarky atheists as the bigger problem?

99. But perhaps most of all: I'm angry because this book touches on—maybe—a hundredth of everything that angers me about religion.

This book barely scratches the surface. I know, almost without a doubt, that within five minutes of it going to press, I'll think of twenty different things I wished I'd put in. This book could easily have been titled, "200 Things That Piss Off the Godless." "500 Things That Piss Off the Godless." "100,000 Things That Piss Off the Godless." I could write an entire encyclopedia on everything about religion that makes me angry... and I still wouldn't be done.

And that seriously pisses me off.

CHAPTER TWO

---✹---

Some Answers to the Questions I Know I'll Get Asked

"But what about…"

Now that you've read my litany of rage, I want to answer some of the questions I know it's going to raise. I know from experience that atheist anger makes emotions run high… and I know what most of the responses to this litany are going to be. So I want to head them off at the pass.

"Your anger is just hurting yourself."

I must respectfully beg to differ. Anger, when it's directed at a real cause of mistreatment or injustice, is healthy, and it can be a useful, constructive motivator to change things. Ask any therapist.

What hurts is repressing anger.

Besides, it's not like I'm angry every second of every day. I wrote this book about some of the things I'm angry about, and that other godless people are angry about. But most of the time, I'm a pretty happy person. I'm good-tempered, cheerful, optimistic, easy to please, and inclined to give people the benefit of the doubt. My life is full of joy and pleasure and weird hobbies: I'm conscious of how fortunate I am; and I make sure to savor my life… especially since I think it's the only one I've got.

Anger is just one part of my emotional makeup. And it's not a bad part. It's possible, even healthy, to be a happy and upbeat person, and still sometimes get angry about things.

Really, I'm fine. This book isn't the only thing I've ever written; it isn't the only thing I'm ever going to write; and it's a little silly to think that it represents my entire philosophy of life. To assume that I, or Richard Dawkins, or PZ Myers, or any other famously "angry atheist," is angry all the time because our angry atheist writing is the only thing people have seen from us… it makes about as much sense as assuming that the only thing Roger Ebert ever does in his entire life is go to the movies. Thank you for your concern, but it's not necessary.

"Your anger is just hurting your cause."

No. You're wrong. Anger is helping our cause. Atheist anger isn't just valid—it's valuable, and it's necessary.

Why?

Because anger is always necessary.

Anger has driven almost every major movement for social change. The labor movement, the civil rights movement, the women's suffrage movement, the modern feminist movement, the gay rights movement, the anti-war movement in the Sixties, the anti-war movement today, the American Revolution itself… all of these have had, as a major driving force, a tremendous amount of anger. And that's just in the United States. Anger has driven social change movements around the world: from the resistance in Nazi Germany to the French Revolution; from the fight against apartheid in South Africa to the fight against fascism in Spain; from the movement against Pinochet in Chile to the Arab Spring uprisings and the anti-theocracy movement in Iran today. Anger over injustice, anger over mistreatment and brutality, anger over helplessness—all of these are powerful inspirations for social change.

I mean, why else would people bother to mobilize social movements? Social movements are hard. They demand time, they demand energy, they sometimes demand serious risk of life and limb, community and career. Nobody would bother if they weren't furious about something.

So when you tell an atheist not to be so angry, you are, in essence, telling us to disempower ourselves. You're telling us to lay down one of the single most powerful tools we have at our disposal. You're telling us to lay down a tool that no social change movement has ever been able to do without. You're telling us to be polite and diplomatic, when history shows that polite diplomacy in a social change movement works far, far better when it's coupled with passionate anger. In a battle between David and Goliath, you're telling David to put down his slingshot and just… I don't know. Gnaw Goliath on the ankles or something.

The belief that "anger doesn't help your cause, anger only alienates people" is a common one. But it's not borne out by history. Anger in a social change movement mobilizes people. It inspires people to action. It gets people off the fence. And it creates visibility for your movement, and awareness of your issues. (I'm always entertained by reporters who ask in bewildered tones, "Why are these people so angry? What do they hope to gain by it?"… when they're featuring them on the nightly news.)

And even the social movement leaders who get tagged as non-angry, peaceful, "good cops" were often very angry indeed. Look at the quotations from Martin Luther King and Gandhi that open this book. These leaders were angry. They championed anger. They simply channeled their anger in constructive ways. Which I think is a grand idea. But acknowledging your anger, and expressing it, is a huge part of that process.

I'll acknowledge that anger is a difficult tool in a social change movement. A dangerous one even. It can make people act rashly; it can make it harder to think clearly; it can make people treat potential allies as enemies. In the worst-case scenario, it can even lead to violence.

Anger is valid, it's valuable and necessary, pretending it doesn't exist does way more harm than expressing it... but it can also misfire, and badly. And contrary to popular opinion, research shows that expressing anger doesn't make people calmer and less angry. Expressing anger actually makes us angrier. So I don't want to be cavalier about anger. I think it's a difficult tool, and one we need to be careful with.

But unless we're endangering or harming somebody, it is not up to believers to tell atheists when we should and should not use this tool. It is not up to believers to tell atheists that we're going too far with the anger and need to calm down. Any more than it's up to white people to say it to black people, or men to say it to women, or straights to say it to queers. When it comes from believers, it's not helpful. It's patronizing. It comes across as another attempt to defang us and shut us up. And it's just going to make us angrier.

"Atheism is just another religion. And you're just as close-minded/faith-based as the believers you criticize."

No, it isn't. And no, I'm not.

It simply isn't the case that atheists are 100% convinced beyond any shadow of a doubt that there is no God. I've met hundreds of atheists—thousands, if you count the ones I've met on the Internet—and I've encountered maybe half a dozen who thought that. (And most of them back down when you press them on it.)

Contrary to popular belief, atheism isn't an unshakeable faith in the non-existence of God. Atheism is... well, it's different for different people. But for most atheists I know, it's more or less the position that the God hypothesis is an extremely unlikely one, not supported by evidence or reason, and that in the absence of any convincing evidence, it's reasonable to discard it. It's the position that the Christian/Judaic/Muslim god is about as probable as Zeus or Thor... and that if you don't believe in those gods, it makes sense to disbelieve in Jehovah/Yahweh/Allah as well. (And the same is true for the Hindu gods, and the Wicca Goddess, and every other god or goddess or supernatural being anyone has ever conceived of. Just while we're at it.)

And it's simply not true that I don't give any reasons for my disbelief, and that I take my disbelief on faith. I've written extensive arguments about why I don't believe in God, or a soul, or an afterlife. As have countless other writers, from Richard Dawkins to Julia Sweeney, Daniel Dennett to Sam Harris. Take a look at The Top Ten Reasons I Don't Believe In God in Chapter Eight, and at the Resource Guide in Chapter Fifteen, if you want to see for yourself.

"Just because religion has done some harm doesn't mean it's mistaken."

You're absolutely right. The good or harm done by religion is irrelevant to whether or not it's true.

It drives me up a tree when religious believers argue for religion by saying how useful it is. The argument from utility—the argument that people should believe in religion because it gives them comfort, because it makes people behave better, because it makes people happy—is absurd on the face of it. The idea of deciding what's true based on what we want to be true is laughable. Or it would be, if it weren't so appalling. I've seen this argument advanced many, many times... and it still shocks me to see otherwise intelligent, thoughtful adults making it. It's preposterous.

But if it's not fair for believers to argue that religion is true because it's useful... then it's equally unfair for atheists to argue that religion is false because it's harmful.

I'm not doing that. These arguments—the argument about whether religion is harmful, and the one about whether religion is true—are two different arguments. They do overlap to some degree: for one thing, many religions offer, as evidence for their particular faith, the notion that people who believe it are doing better in their lives than people who don't. And the fact that religion is mistaken makes it inherently more likely to do harm: decisions based on false assumptions are more likely to get screwed up. But basically, you're right. Religion could be harmful, and still be true.

And I care passionately about what is and is not true.

That's not the focus of this particular book. The main focus of this book is why religion sucks and why so many atheists are pissed off about it. But this pesky question of whether or not God exists? It's relevant, and it's important. So I do spend some time here making a summary of my case for atheism. My Top Ten Reasons I Don't Believe In God can be found in Chapter Eight. (You can find a list of more exhaustive arguments against religion, by myself and other atheist writers, in the Resource Guide at the end of this book.)

"All religion isn't like that. You're not being fair. It's just a few bad apples. You're painting us all with the same brush."

I'm not.

I'm careful in this book to say, "I'm angry at people who do (X)," or, "I get angry when (Y) happens," or, "I'm angry about (Z)." I say that I'm angry about specific aspects of religion, specific ways it plays out in the world, specific things people do because of their religion.

But the stuff I'm angry about is not a few bad apples. I'm sorry, but that's just flat-out wrong. Do you seriously think that 53% of Americans refusing to vote for an atheist under any circumstances is a few bad apples? A national public health and sex education policy based on unproven and unprovable religious doctrine instead of actual evidence? The Catholic Church's policy of opposing condom distribution? The fact that until the year I was born, the law in many states said that atheists couldn't vote or hold office or testify in court?

Those are not bad apples. That is widespread, systematic religious oppression. The stuff I'm angry about may not be universal, but it is not unusual. It's depressingly common. The stuff in this book may not be true for you and your church, synagogue, mosque, coven, etc. If so, good for you. But it's still important, still widespread, and still worth being angry about. And it's totally screwed-up to dismiss it as a trivial aspect of religion, simply because it isn't universal.

And in fact, I would argue that, even if your particular religion hasn't done these particular things, it still causes harm. I think religion, by its very nature, is a bad idea that does significantly more harm than good. I'll explain why, in Chapter Three: Why This Really Is Religion's Fault.

"All believers aren't like that. That's not the true faith."

You're trying to piss me off now, aren't you?

Okay. Deep breaths. (*Calm blue ocean, calm blue ocean…*)

Go back and read #94 and #95 in the Litany. The part about the "true faith" thing and how messed-up it is. The part about how nobody has a pipeline to God. The part about how you have no more reason than anyone else to think you know what God wants. (I also get into this more in Chapter Four: "Yes, This Means You: Moderate and Progressive Religion.")

And when it comes to Christianity specifically: I'm sorry, but the whole "Jesus was a cool guy who gets misinterpreted by those organized religion fascists" thing? It ignores the actual content of the Gospels. If you believe that the Gospels are a more or less accurate representation of what Jesus said, you have to acknowledge that this Jesus guy said some pretty screwed-up stuff.[1] Including a whole lot of stuff about how people who didn't believe in him and follow him were going to burn in Hell for eternity.[2]

The thing you need to remember is this: You don't have any more reason to think you have the true faith than any other believer does. Sure, you can quote chapter and verse—and so can people with a different interpretation of the faith. That's the nature of chapter and verse; it can be used to support just about any interpretation you can come up with. Even if God exists, you don't have a pipeline to him, and you don't know what he wants any more than anyone else.

Besides, see above about the "few bad apples." Even if the way you practice religion is reasonably cool, there are still widespread, systematic practices of religion that aren't so cool. And even if you don't agree with them, they still count as religion.

"How can you be so hateful? You're speaking out against hatred... and yet you're so full of hate yourself."

I'm not.

In the entirety of this book, I used the word "hate" exactly three times... and it's all in one paragraph. It's in the paragraph that reads, "I'm angry that children get taught by religion to hate and fear their bodies and their sexuality. And I'm especially angry that female children get taught by religion to hate and fear their femaleness, and that queer children get taught by religion to hate and fear their queerness." In this entire book, the only time I use the word "hate" (other than quotations or citations of other people) is to speak out against it.

I never once, in this entire book, say that I hate anyone. I say that I'm angry. There's an enormous difference.

"But the people who perpetrate religion's harms are also being injured by it. How can you be angry at them? Where's your compassion?"

Yes. This is true. And it's one of the things that makes anger about religion complicated. The people who perpetrate religion's horrors are, for the most part, also its victims. And vice versa. The people who traumatize their young children with vivid and horrific images of Hell were, themselves, traumatized by those horrors. The religious leaders who fill their flocks with close-minded ignorance and hateful bigotry were, themselves, taught that ignorance and bigotry are divine virtues, treasured by God. The people who are warping the sexuality of their kids and teenagers, filling them with guilt and shame over normal healthy feelings, were, themselves, warped in this same way.

This doesn't make me less passionate about my atheist activism. It makes me more passionate.

When I see religion as a continually self-perpetuating chain of victimization and perpetration, it makes me both angrier and more compassionate. It makes me feel more compassion for religious people—and more anger about religion. And it inspires me to work even harder to create a world without religion. It inspires me to make my arguments against religion stronger... so more people will be persuaded out of it. It inspires me to make the atheist community healthier... so more people will feel safe and welcome in it. It inspires me to make atheism more visible... so more people will see it as an option. It inspires me to make atheism persuasive, and inviting, and impossible to ignore... so more people will reconsider their religion, earlier in their lives, when there's a better chance for the cycle to be broken.

"People need religion. It's not going anywhere. You're wishing for something that's never, ever going to happen."

I suppose that's possible. I don't think we have any way of knowing that yet. Godlessness has only fairly recently become an acceptable option in human society—and in much of the world, it still isn't.

But we do have one experimental Petri dish... and it shows this argument to be hogwash. I offer as a counter example: Europe.

Many European nations are now more than half atheist/agnostic. In some cases, significantly more. And those nations are doing fine. Much better than countries with a high number of believers, in fact. According to *Society without God: What the Least Religious Nations Can Tell Us About Contentment* by Phil Zuckerman, countries with high rates of atheism tend to be the happiest and highest-functioning countries we have. Their residents score at the very top of the "happiness index," and their societies boast some of the lowest rates of violent crime in the world, some of the lowest levels of corruption, excellent educational systems, strong economies, well-supported arts, free health care, egalitarian social policies, and more.

And while I think the cause and effect works in the other direction—greater social health leads to more godlessness, not the other way around—the fact that there are flourishing countries with a godless majority puts the kibosh on the whole "religion is a basic human need" theory. These countries aren't perfect, they have their problems; but no more than we do in the U.S., and in many ways a lot less. It's pretty clear that, once basic human needs for food/shelter/health care/ ducation/social justice are fairly well met, people lose their need for religion.

"Why do you care what other people believe? Why can't you just live and let live?"

Did you read the last chapter?

That entire chapter is an explanation of why I care. Heck, this entire book is an explanation of why I care. I care because far too many believers aren't living and letting live. I care because people act on their beliefs. I care because people's beliefs lead them to do terrible harm to other people, and to themselves. I care because the whole "faith trumps evidence" aspect of religion makes it uniquely resistant to self-correction… and uniquely resistant to dissent.

Of course people are entitled to believe what they want. It's a right guaranteed in the Constitution, and it's a right that I treasure passionately. But nowhere in the Constitution does it say that the right to believe whatever you want means that nobody should ever argue with you or point out why they think you're mistaken. Somehow, the very good concept of religious tolerance got turned into the very bad concept that nobody should say anything critical of any religion, ever.

Yes, people have a right to not vote for atheists. They also have a right to not vote for blacks or women or Jews. Does that make what they're doing okay? Does that mean we shouldn't try to change their minds? Does that mean we shouldn't be angry about it?

"You're trying to force your beliefs on me. You're just as intolerant as the intolerant believers you're criticizing."

I'm forcing my beliefs on you… how? By speaking about them? By blogging about them? By writing a book about them?

Nowhere in this book, or anywhere in my writing, do I advocate preventing people from practicing their religious beliefs. I am a staunch, almost rabid supporter of the First Amendment… and that includes both the part about the government not establishing a religion, *and* the part about the government not prohibiting the free exercise thereof. In fact, many of my most gut-wrenching rages about religion are on behalf of religious believers, who face abuse and injustice and persecution at the hands of other believers with more clout.

Yes, I oppose things like public school teachers preaching in the classroom. But that's because I *do* support religious freedom—and I therefore don't want government promoting one religion over another. That's something religious believers often forget: Separation of church and state doesn't just work for atheists. It works for believers. Imagine that in your town, people of a radically different faith from yours started flocking in from around the country, and within a few months they were in the majority. Would you want their god prayed to at your city council meetings? Would you want their religion taught to your kids in the public schools? Would you want their holy texts posted in your courthouse? If not—then please shut the hell up about how keeping religion out of government is a horrible form of religious repression.

And yes, I'll be honest: I'd like to see humanity let go of religion. I think it's a mistaken idea about the world; I think it's an idea that, on the whole, does more harm than good; and I'd like to see people abandon it. But I absolutely do not want that to happen by force. I would vehemently oppose any attempts to make it happen by force. And I don't know any other atheists who want it to happen by force. I want to see it happen by persuasion.

But please see "Why do you care what other people believe?" above. Religious tolerance is not the same as never criticizing religion, or asking hard questions about it.

Religion has gotten a free ride in the marketplace of ideas for far too long. Religion is a hypothesis about the world: a theory of how the world works and how we should behave in it. So it's reasonable to question it, to debate it, to point out when it doesn't fit the evidence or doesn't make sense. That's not intolerance. And it's not forcing ideas on anybody. We criticize every other kind of idea: we criticize ideas about science, politics, philosophy, medicine, art, public policy, pop culture, and who had the best Red Carpet look at the Golden Globes. Why, alone among all other ideas that humanity has come up with, does religion get to be free from criticism and questioning and mockery? Why, alone among all other ideas, does religion get a free ride in the marketplace of ideas? In an armored car? Why does it get to sell its wares behind a curtain? And why is it so terrible to hand out flyers in the market saying that the teakettles we bought from religion don't hold water? What makes religion so different, so special, that it deserves this kid-gloves treatment?

I have asked this question more times than I can remember, of more religious believers than I can count. And I have never once gotten a satisfactory answer. In fact, most of the time I never get any answer at all. I've only gotten an answer once, from a believer who replied that historically, religious debates and differences have repeatedly turned into hatred and violent conflict, so they ought to be avoided entirely. Which actually proves my point and not his: religion is a bad idea, and humanity should abandon it.

"What about all the good things religion has done?"

What about them?

Yes, Martin Luther King, Jr. Yes, Gandhi. Yes, the Catholic Workers. I'm not arguing that religion is universally and uniformly harmful and never useful for anyone, and always has been throughout history. I'm arguing that religion, on the whole, more often than not, for more people than not, does more harm than good. I'm arguing that most, if not all, of the good it gives can be gained in other ways, from other sources of community and philosophy and social support and so on. I'm arguing that, on balance, the limited good that religion provides is not worth it.

Yes, religion has occasionally done some good. But it's also done terrible, appalling, nightmarishly evil harm. And atheists are bloody well going to speak out about it.

"You wouldn't be so angry if you just accepted Jesus Christ as your personal savior."

Now you're definitely trying to piss me off.

Okay. First of all, see above, about how I'm not angry every second of every day. And also about occasional anger being a healthy part of life.

Second: Do you honestly think I've never heard this before? Do you think that, in over fifty years of being on this planet, and over seven years of being an atheist blogger, nobody before has ever said to me, "Everything in your life would improve if you just accepted Jesus Christ as your personal savior"? Yes, I've read the Bible (much of it, anyway). I was a religion major in college. I've considered the possibility that Jesus might be my personal savior. And I've rejected it. The evidence supporting the "Jesus is my personal savior" hypothesis is pathetically weak at best, flat-out laughable at worst. If you don't have any good evidence supporting this hypothesis, don't waste my time with it. Please. Come up with something new.

And third... do you think there are no angry Christians in the world? I see angry Christians everywhere. America is full of Christians who are full of anger—hatred, even—for homosexuals, feminists, liberals, sex educators, and so on. (In other words... for me.)

When I wrote the blog post that this book was based on, I got comments[3] from believers who said I shouldn't be allowed to vote or serve on juries; that I was angry because I was a lesbo bulldyke; that they wished my mother had had an abortion and I should burn in Hell. I got a comment from a believer who told me to drink bleach. Christianity is no cure for anger. Christianity often serves to fan anger's flame.

"I'm an atheist—and I'm not angry about any of this. You don't speak for me."

Okay.

I don't claim to speak every godless person on the planet. I'm mostly speaking for myself. If I'm not speaking for you, fine. I'm not pretending to.

But I know—from the overwhelming response I got when I first blogged about this, from the overwhelming response I get when I speak on this topic—that I speak for a lot of people. The number of people who email me, or comment on my blog, or come up to me after my talks, to say, "You said exactly what I think but can't say," or, "I'm bookmarking this so I can link to it every time someone asks me what I'm angry about"... well, I haven't counted them, but it's freaking huge.

"I'm a believer—and I'm angry about this stuff, too."

Good. You should be.

I'm not trying to argue that this litany of anger is limited to the godless. Many religious believers get just as angry as atheists about religious intolerance and oppression. Some of them even more so, since the intolerant oppressive stuff makes them look bad. And that's exactly as it should be.

I still think you're mistaken about this god stuff. But that doesn't mean we can't be allies.

"If you're so angry, what are you doing about it?"

Mostly, I'm writing. I'm a writer. That's what I do. I change people's minds. I persuade people that religion is mistaken. I inspire people to get off the fence about their lack of belief. I give people ideas and language they can carry into their own debates with believers. I give people ideas on how to live a happy godless life. I discuss strategy for the atheist movement. I inspire atheists to come out of the closet.

I do other things as well. I travel around the country doing public speaking about atheism. I promote other atheist writers. I strategize with other atheist activists. I donate money. I do fundraising for atheist organizations and causes. I write to my Congresspeople. I pay attention to these issues when I vote.

But mostly, I'm writing. I'm a writer. That's what I do.

"I'm angry, too. What can I do about it?"

Take a look at the resource guide at the end of this book. It lists organizations, online forums, books, blogs, activist groups, etc., where you can go to get information and join communities and take action.

But most importantly: You can come out. You can tell your friends, your families, your co-workers, your bowling league, everyone. I said it earlier, but it's important, and I'm going to say it again: Coming out is the single most effective political action a godless person can take. Coming out is how we counter the myths and misinformation people have about us. It's how we become a political force to be reckoned with. It's how we become a vocal movement that people are afraid to antagonize. It's how we become a voting bloc. And it's how we deny the social consent that religion relies on to perpetuate itself. The more of us who say out loud, "The Emperor has no clothes," the easier it becomes for other atheists to speak out... and the harder it gets for believers to keep convincing themselves that they're seeing something that isn't there.

If there is any way that you can take this step without screwing up your life—please, please do it. Come out, come out, wherever you are.

CHAPTER THREE

---✸---

Why This Really Is Religion's Fault

"Okay," you might be saying now. "Yes. All of that is terrible. No sane person could read that litany of rage, and think any of it was anything other than appalling. But these evils aren't religion's fault! People do terrible things to each other for all sorts of reasons. Greed, fear, selfishness, the hunger for power, the desire for control… all these things lead people to do evil. And people come up with all sorts of rationalizations for the terrible things they do. You can't blame religion for all the terrible things done in its name."

If you're saying that… you might be surprised to hear me say this, but I think you have a point. I ultimately don't agree with you—but you have a serious point, and it needs to be addressed.

I'm not saying that religion is the root of all evil. I'm not arguing that a world without religion would be a blissful Utopia where everyone holds hands and chocolate flows in the streets. (And then we all die, because the chocolate is drowning us and we can't swim because we're holding hands.) I don't know of any atheist who'd argue that. I know that the impulses driving evil are deeply rooted in human nature. Religion is far from the only motivation for human evil, and it's far from the only excuse for it.

But I would argue that religion is unique. And I would argue that the things that make religion unique also make it uniquely capable of causing terrible harm.

So what is it about religion—exactly—that's so harmful? Sure, I can make a list of harms religion has done, from here to Texas. I've done just that, right up front in Chapter One. But that's not enough to make my case. I could make long lists of harms done by plenty of human institutions: medicine, education, democracy. That doesn't make them inherently malevolent.

Why is religion special—and specially troubling? What makes religion different from any other ideology, community, system of morality, hypothesis about how the world works? And why does that difference make it uniquely prone to causing damage?

I don't have ten arguments for why religion is harmful. I don't even have 99 arguments.

I have one.

Everything I've ever written about religion's harm boils down to one thing. It's this:

Religion is a belief in invisible beings, inaudible voices, intangible entities, undetectable forces, and events and judgments that happen after we die.

It therefore has no reality check.

After all, religion isn't the only belief that's armored against criticism, questioning, and self-correction. It is uniquely armored against anything that might stop it from spinning into extreme absurdity, extreme denial of reality… and extreme, grotesque immorality.

I can hear the chorus already. "But not all religion is like that! Not all believers are crazy extremists! Some religions adapt to new evidence and changing social mores! It's not fair to criticize all religion just because some believers do bad things!" I hear you. I'll get to that, here, and in the chapters that follow. First , hear me out.

The Proof Is Not in the Pudding

The thing that uniquely defines religion, the thing that sets it apart from every other hypothesis or ideology or social network, is the belief in unverifiable supernatural entities. Of course it has other elements—community, charity, philosophy, inspiration for art, etc. But these exist in the secular world, too. They're not specific to religion. The thing that uniquely defines religion is belief in supernatural entities. Without that belief, it's not religion.

And with that belief, the capacity for religion to do harm gets cranked up to an alarmingly high level—because there's no reality check.

Any other ideology or philosophy or hypothesis about the world is eventually expected to pony up. It's expected to prove itself true, or else correct itself, or else fall by the wayside. With religion, that is emphatically not the case. Because religion is a belief in the invisible and unknowable—and it's therefore never expected to prove that it's right, or even show good evidence for why it's right—its capacity to do harm can spin into the stratosphere.

Let me make a comparison to show my point. Let's compare religious belief with political ideology. After all, religion isn't the only belief that's armored against criticism, questioning, and self-correction. Religion isn't the only belief that leads people to ignore evidence in favor of their settled opinion. And contrary to the popular atheist saying, religion is not the only belief that inspires good people to do evil things. Political ideology can do all of that. People committed horrors to perpetuate Soviet Communism: an ideology many of those people sincerely believed was best. And horrors were committed by Americans in the last Bush administration… in the name of democracy and freedom.

But even the most stubborn political ideology will eventually crumble in the face of it, you know, not working. People can only be told for so long that under Communism everyone will eat strawberries and cream, or that in an unrestricted free market the rising tide will lift all boats. A political ideology makes promises about this life, this world. If the strawberries and cream and rising boats aren't forthcoming, eventually people notice. (The U.S. Presidential election of 2008 was evidence of that.) People can rationalize a political ideology for a long time... but ultimately, the proof is in the pudding.

Religion is different.

With religion, the proof is emphatically not in the pudding. With religion, the proof comes from invisible beings, inaudible voices. The proof comes from prophets and religious leaders, who supposedly hear these voices and are happy to tell the rest of us what they say. It comes from religious texts, written ages ago by prophets and religious leaders, who were just as happy back then to tell people about the inaudible voices as religious leaders are today. It comes from feelings in people's hearts that, conveniently, tell them what they already believe or want to believe. And the proof comes in the afterlife, after people die and can't tell us about it. Every single claim made by religion comes from people: not from sources out in the world that other people can verify, but from the insides of people's heads.

So with religion, even if God's rules and promises aren't working out, followers still follow them... because the ultimate judge and judgment are invisible. There is no pudding, no proof—and no expectation that there should be any. And there is therefore no reality check, no self-correction, when religion starts to go to the bad place.

In fact, with many religions, that idea that you should expect to eat the pudding is blasphemy. A major part of many religious doctrines is that trusting the tenets of your faith without evidence is not only acceptable, but a positive virtue. ("Have you believed because you have seen me? Blessed are those who have not seen and yet believe." —John 20:29)

In other words: The belief in invisible beings, undetectable forces, and events that happen after we die, provides a uniquely effective armor against the valid criticism, questioning, and dismantling of ideas and institutions that do serious harm.

And religion builds on this armor with layer after layer. Among these insulating layers: The idea that letting go of religious doubts is a liberating act of love. The idea that skepticism and questioning are the same as cynicism, nihilism, and despair. The idea that religion operates in a different realm from the everyday world, and it's unfair to hold it to normal standards of evidence. The idea that criticizing religion is rude and intolerant. The "Shut up, that's why"[4] arguments so commonly marshaled against atheists: arguments meant not to address questions about religion, but to silence them. When coupled with the fact that the core belief is by definition unverifiable, these layers armor religion even more effectively against valid questions… thus undermining our ability to see when it's become comically absurd, or wildly implausible, or grotesquely immoral. Or all three.

I want to give some specific examples of how this armor works. I want to talk about some of the most common—and most harmful—ways that religion causes harm. And I want to show how the invisible, unprovable, "don't show me the money" nature of religion either directly causes that harm or makes it worse.

Inspiring political oppression. Religious extremists—whether the Taliban in the Islamic world or the Christian Right in the United States—don't care about separation of church and state. They don't care about democracy. They don't care about respecting other people's right to live differently from them. In the most extreme cases, they don't care about law, or basic principles of morality, or even human life.

None of this matters to them. What matters is making God's will happen. In their minds, God created everything that exists, and God controls everything that exists… and therefore, God's will trumps everything.

And since God's will is invisible, inaudible, and unverifiable, there's no reality check on this dreadful path. There's no reality check saying that their actions are having a terrible effect in the world around them. The world around them is, quite literally, irrelevant. The next world is what matters. And since there's no way to conclusively demonstrate what will and won't get you a good place in that next world, or whether it even exists… the sky's the limit. There's no way to test the assertion that God wants women to wear burqas and have clitoridectomies… or that God wants us to ban same-sex marriage and teach children dangerous lies about sex. The reality check is absent. The brake lines of morality have been cut.

Perpetuating political oppression. The unverifiability of religion leads to political oppression in another way. It makes religious leaders and organizations uniquely powerful in the political arena—because their followers are typically taught from a young age to believe whatever their religious leaders say. They are taught that their religious leaders have superior virtue, with a hotline to God and his all-perfect morality. Indeed, they've been taught that trusting their religious leaders is a virtue, and that asking them to support their claims with evidence is a grave insult: not only to the leaders, but to the entire faith, and even to God himself.

So when religious leaders step into the political arena and teach that political oppression is God's will, the healthy suspicion and skepticism that politicians are typically met with get abandoned. These leaders can say and do whatever they want, and people will believe them. There's no reality check.

I want to give a specific example of this one. I want to talk about same-sex marriage.

In the United States, whenever same-sex marriage has been up for popular vote, it has, as of this writing, never won. It's won in legislatures and in the judiciary—but it has been consistently defeated at the ballot box, even when a well-organized, well-funded campaign has been behind it. It has been defeated at the ballot box—largely because the full force of several organized religions, particularly the Catholic and Mormon churches, have been marshaled against it. It has been defeated because these churches have been willing to tell grotesque, shameless lies about the effects of same-sex marriage—from "churches will be forced to perform weddings they oppose" to "kids will be taught explicit gay sex in public school."

And it has been defeated because the followers of these churches implicitly trust their leaders. When faced with a newspaper editorial saying, "Same-sex marriage won't affect public education"—and their beloved priest saying, "Same-sex marriage means your children will be taught about gay oral sex in third grade"—they believe their priest.

Even though their priest is lying through his teeth.

And because religion has no reality check, it is extraordinarily difficult to counter its leaders' flat-out lies... because their claims rest on an unverifiable belief in an invisible god, who has yet to appear on CNN stating his political views. And when you combine this lack of reality check with the unquestioning trust in religious leaders, you have a recipe for religion to have grossly disproportionate power in the political arena. A power that is uniquely armored against questions about what actually works to improve life and alleviate suffering and create justice in this world. You know. The questions that politics are supposed to be about.

Succumbing to political oppression. In the same way that religion's unverifiability means there's no check on oppressing other people, it means there's no check on people accepting their own oppression. At the hands of religion, or anything else.

If people believe they'll be rewarded with infinite bliss in the afterlife—and there's no way to prove whether or not that's true—people will let themselves be martyrs to their faith, to an appalling degree. More commonly, if people believe in infinite bliss in the afterlife, they'll be more willing to accept an appalling degree of oppression and injustice in this life. From anybody.

Oddly, this is often framed as a plus. "Religion gives people hope in hardship." It gets presented as a feature, not a bug. But I fail to see how encouraging oppressed people to suck it up until they get pie in the sky is a good thing. (For the oppressed, anyway. Why it's good for the oppressors is crystal clear.)

Again: Because it's a belief in invisible beings and judgments that happen after people die, religion short-circuits our reality checks. Including the reality check that looks at how we're being treated and says, "This is bullshit."

Individual abuses by religious leaders. This one should be obvious. But it's important, and I want to spell it out.

The same forces that give religious leaders disproportionate power in politics also give them disproportionate power in people's personal lives. When people are taught that religious leaders have a unique hotline to God's morality, they're more inclined to trust them without question. And that can lead to disaster.

Sexual abuse of children is the most obvious example. Children's natural tendency to trust and obey adults—a tendency that can be abused by any authority figure—is multiplied a hundredfold when that authority seems to come from God himself.

But it's not the only example. When the promise of infinite bliss in the next life is held out like a carrot dangled before a donkey's nose—and there's no way to know if the carrot is even there—people will let themselves be taken advantage of by religious leaders to an appalling degree.

And even if an individual believer decides, "Hey, wait a minute! It isn't okay that the leader bilked me out of my life savings, or used the hospital fund to buy a Bentley, or molested me at age seven"... who's going to believe them? Religion's armor against criticism means that even when someone begins to doubt, others in their belief community keep believing. And those others will reject any accusations made against the leader… no matter how credible, or how well supported by evidence. The armor of God doesn't just make believers vulnerable to religious leaders' fraud and abuse. It ensures that if they do wise up to that fraud and abuse, their accusations won't be believed.

Justification for bigotry. Human beings don't need religious justification for bigotry. We can be bigoted just fine on our own. But as powerful as bigotry is, it does have a natural, if painfully slow, reality check. When people see that in reality, not all women are ditzy idiots, and not all black people are lazy criminals, and not all gay people are miserable and crazy… eventually, over years and decades, they can change their minds. (And if they don't, their kids do. The strongest determining factor in whether Americans support same-sex marriage is youth.) Bigotry is strong… but reality, plus time, is stronger.

But when bigotry is justified by religion, this reality check gets shot in the foot. When bigotry is justified by the inaudible voice of God— and by the very audible voices of people claiming to speak for God— the reality check saying that bigotry isn't right gets easily drowned out.

Again, because the voice of God is inaudible, and the proof of the pudding is in the afterlife where nobody can see it… well, if it's God telling you that blacks were condemned by God to serve whites, or that women were designed by God to defer to men, or that homosexuals have abandoned morality and defied God's will, who are you to say it isn't true? Sure, you have the reality of good gays and independent women and brilliant black people with outstanding leadership skills… but balance that against the word of the creator of the Universe, and what's going to win?

Especially when it's a bigotry you're already inclined to believe, and one that works in your favor? When bigotry is justified by the untestable voice of religious faith, what chance does inconvenient reality have?

Justification for violence and war. Ditto. But more so. In the same way that religion drowns out the reality check saying that bigotry and oppression is wrong, it drowns out the reality check saying that hurting and killing people is wrong.

And the untestable belief in the afterlife is the biggest obstacle to this reality check. If you believe in a perfect eternal afterlife... then who cares about pain and death in this world? Compared with the eternal bliss/torture of Heaven or Hell, pain and death in this world is a stubbed toe. Isn't carrying out God's will more important than a stubbed toe?

Kill them all. Let God sort it out.

Vulnerability to fraud. When people are taught that believing things without proof or evidence makes you a good person, they become far more vulnerable to fraud, manipulation, and deception.

Not just from religious figures. Not just from phony faith healers and prosperity gospel preachers and authors of bestselling psychic self-help books. From everybody. From every Ponzi schemer and Nigerian email scammer and shady purveyor of Florida real estate.

When people are taught to let go of difficult questions and trust whatever religious authorities tell them? That it's better to trust their feelings than their critical thinking skills? That evidence and reason are less important than faith? That "doubter" is a synonym for "sinner"? They become vulnerable to every cheater, chiseler, swindler, con artist, and late night infomercial huckster who's lucky enough to cross their gullible paths. This idea that belief without evidence is a virtue... it doesn't just inspire people to trust their religious leaders blindly. It inspires people to trust *anybody* blindly. Including people who are trying to rob them blind.

Quashing science and education. Do I even need to explain this one? Do I need to explain how the untestability of religion— and the idea that untestability is a positive virtue—undercuts science and education? Not just in a general, "making people devalue science and education" way—but in specific, practical, harmful ways? Hamstringing stem cell research? Forcing abstinence-only sex education on kids? Teaching creationism in public schools?

When religion teaches that believing in the invisible is more important than understanding the perceivable… that personal faith is more important than critical thinking… that letting go of questions is a liberating act of love and trust… that believing things with no evidence is not only okay but a positive virtue… that unfalsifiable hypotheses are just ducky… that what God supposedly says about the world is more real than what's in the world itself…

Do I need to explain this any further? Do I need to explain how this "Facts take a back seat to faith" trope hammers science and education into the ground?

Quashing medicine and public health. Ditto "Quashing science and education." But with this addition:

Religion, and its unverifiability, promotes the idea that the invisible afterlife is more important than this life, the one we know exists. And it therefore promotes the idea that even if a medical treatment or health policy would reduce disease and death, it doesn't matter. Even though condoms help prevent the spread of AIDS, even though immunizing girls against genital warts helps prevent cervical cancer, even though stem cell research could lead to great advances in medicine… it doesn't matter. What matters isn't disease and death in this life. What matters is the next life. What matters is God's will.

Which, again, we have no way of verifying. And which therefore, by the horrible freakish paradox of the armor of God, gets priority.

Terrorizing children. And again, we come to the matter of priorities.

If we prioritized this life, we would never terrorize children by telling them they'll be tortured in fire forever if they don't obey our rules. We would never tell them to imagine putting their hands in a fire, to imagine the crackling and burning and screaming pain… and then to imagine doing that for a minute. An hour. A day. A lifetime. Eternity.

Not unless we were horribly abusive.

But when people think that the next life is more important than this one—when people think that the infinite burning and torture is genuinely going to happen if their children don't obey God's word—they'll gladly give their children nightmarish visions of pain and torture, dispensed by the fatherly god who supposedly created them and loves them. They'll do it without a second thought. When people prioritize their belief in an afterlife that, by definition, is impossible to prove or disprove, they cut the reality check that's telling them—no, that's begging them—not to terrorize and emotionally abuse their own children.

Teaching children about Hell is child abuse. Nothing but the unverifiable promise of permanent bliss or torture in the afterlife would make loving, decent, non-abusive parents inflict it on their children.

I could go on, and on, and on. But I think you get the idea.

Now, many believers will argue that the harm done by religion isn't religion's fault. Many believers will point out all the wars, bigotry, fraud, oppression, quashing of science and medicine, and terrorizing of children done for reasons other than religion. Many will argue that, even when this horrible stuff is done in the name of religion, it isn't inspired by religion at all. It's inspired by greed, fear, selfishness, the hunger for power, the desire for control… all the things that lead people to do evil. And many will point out that not all religions are the extremist variety that leads people to commit atrocities and deny reality.

And again I'll say: Yes, you have a point. It would be simplistic to argue that religion is the root of all evil, or to deny the role that money and power and tribalism and other human tendencies play in religious hatred and conflict. I know that the impulses driving evil are deeply rooted in human nature, and religion is far from the only thing to inspire it.

I'm saying that religion provides a uniquely stubborn justification for evil. I'm saying that religion is uniquely armored against criticism, questioning, and self-correction... and that this armor protects it against the reality checks that act, to a limited degree and in the long run, to keep evil in check. I'm saying that religion takes the human impulses towards evil, and cuts the brake line, and sends them careening down a hill and into the center of town.

Without religion, we would still have community. Charity. Social responsibility. Philosophy. Ethics. Comfort. Solace. Art. In countries where less than half the population believes in God, these qualities and activities are all flourishing. In fact, they're flourishing far more than they are in countries with high rates of religious belief.

We don't need religion to have any of these things.

And we'd be better off without it.

CHAPTER FOUR

Yes, This Means You: Moderate and Progressive Religion

"But surely you don't mean progressive and moderate religion! You're talking about the fundamentalists, the extremists, the Taliban, the hard-core Religious Right. But that's not true Christianity, true Judaism, true Islam, true whatever. Of course you're angry about that stuff. But I'm a progressive believer! I support gay rights! I support separation of church and state! I support science—I don't think it has to be in conflict with religion! I'm tolerant and accepting of other religions! When you talk about what makes atheists mad about religion... surely you don't mean me?"

Actually—yes, I do mean you.

Okay. I'll modify that a bit. I'm not as angry about progressive and moderate religion as I am about the extremist varieties. If all religion were moderate, ecumenical, separate from government, supportive of science, and accepting of non-belief... well, atheists would still disagree with it, but most of us wouldn't much care.

But moderate and progressive religion still does harm. And it still pisses me off.

Moderate and progressive religion still encourages people to believe in invisible beings, inaudible voices, intangible entities, undetectable forces, and events and judgments that happen after we die. And therefore, it still disables reality checks… making people more vulnerable to oppression, fraud, and abuse.

And moderate and progressive religion still encourages the basic idea of faith: the idea that it's acceptable, and even virtuous, to believe things you have no good reason to think are true. I can't count the number of times I've heard moderate and progressive believers say how wonderful it is to think with your heart and not your head; how we need religion to preserve the mystery of life; how an excessive concern with reason and evidence closes you off to the grander truths of the Universe. Moderate and progressive religion encourages the idea that it's acceptable, even virtuous, to prioritize wishful thinking over reality. It encourages the idea that it's acceptable, even virtuous, to give greater importance to the world inside your head than you do to the vast world outside of it. It encourages the idea that it's acceptable, even virtuous, to ignore reality when we're making important decisions that affect ourselves and others.

And that, in and of itself, is a disturbing and dangerous idea.

Let's make an analogy. Let's pretend there are people who are convinced that they get instructions on how to live, not from God, but from their hair dryer. Let's say that Person 1 thinks their hair dryer is telling them to shoot every redhead who gets on the 9:04 train. And let's say Person 2 thinks their hair dryer is telling them to volunteer twice a week at a homeless shelter.

Is it better to volunteer at a homeless shelter than it is to shoot every redhead who gets on the 9:04 train? Of course it is.

But you still have a basic problem—which is that you think your hair dryer is talking to you.

You are still getting your ethics from a hair dryer. You are still getting your perception of reality and your ideas about how to live your life, not from the core moral values that most human beings seem to share, not from any solid evidence about what decreases suffering and increases fairness and happiness, not from your own experience of what makes the world a better place... but from a household appliance.

And that's a problem. It's a problem for what I hope is an obvious reason: Hair dryers don't talk to us. Thinking that they do is out of touch with reality. And I hope I don't have to explain why we should care about reality, and about whether the things we believe are true.

But it's also a problem because, if you think your hair dryer is a valid source of moral guidance... what do you do if it starts telling you something different? Something less noble than "volunteer at the homeless shelter twice a week"? Something absurd (and not in a good way); something self-destructive; something grossly immoral?

What do you do if your hair dryer starts telling you to go to your blind date wearing a wedding dress and a hat made from a rubber chicken? What do you do if your hair dryer starts telling you, not just to volunteer at the homeless shelter twice a week, but to donate your entire paycheck to the homeless shelter, every week, to the point where you become homeless yourself? What do you do if your hair dryer starts telling you to shoot every redhead who gets on the 9:04 train?

If you don't have a better reason for what you do than, "The hair dryer told me to," you're in trouble. You have no reality check on your perceptions or ideas or decisions. And if you do have a better reason for what you do than, "The hair dryer told me to"... then why do you need the hair dryer?

So yes. If you're volunteering at a homeless shelter twice a week, you're doing better than the person who shoots every redhead on the 9:04 train. But if you're getting your ideas about reality and morality from a household appliance... then you've got a problem.

And if you're getting your ideas about reality and morality from an invisible being who nobody can agree about and who you have no good reason to think even exists... then you've got a problem.

Faith without evidence is a bad idea. It's a bad idea to believe things you have no good reason to think are true. Even if it sometimes leads to good conclusions; even if it's moderate and tolerant... it's still a bad idea. Period.

What's more: Moderate religion is in the minority. The oppressive, intolerant, reality-denying forms of religion are far more common, and far better at perpetuating themselves. And moderate religion gives these ugly forms credibility. It gives credibility to the idea that faith—i.e., believing in things you have no good reason to think are true—is valid, and indeed virtuous. It gives credibility to the idea that invisible worlds are real: not only real, but more real, and more important, than the visible world. It gives credibility to the idea that our profoundly biased intuition is more trustworthy than logic or verifiable evidence. It gives credibility to the idea that religious beliefs, alone among all other ideas, should be beyond criticism, and that the very act of questioning religion is inherently intolerant. (And when questioned even a little by non-believers, its adherents tend to get decidedly hostile and un-moderate.)

As for that whole "they're not true Christians" thing...

Progressive Christians love to say that extremist bigotry and hateful hellfire isn't Christian. "The true message of Jesus is compassion and tolerance," they'll say. "The true message of Jesus is loving your neighbor. What the Christian Right does and says—that's not true Christianity."

And they're just as full of it as the Christian Right.

I obviously agree with them about the actual issues. Bigoted theocracy—boo. Love and tolerance and being nice to gay people—yay. The progressive view of Christ's message is a better one. It's just not a more Christian one.

Of course the progressives and moderates can quote chapter and verse to support their flavor of Christianity. But the Christian Right can do that, too. It's easy to find hellfire and intolerant judgment[5] in the Bible, even in the Gospels. There are, by my count, thirty-seven places in the Gospels[6] where the Jesus character explicitly refers to the concept of Hell. And that doesn't count the more indirect implications and allusions. The references aren't out of context, either: they're woven throughout the text, with several consistent themes emerging, such as people being damned to Hell for hearing Jesus and still not believing. It's not a tangential concept—it's front and center.

And yes, the Christian Right cherry-picks the parts of Scripture that support their vision, and ignores the parts that don't. Which is exactly what progressive Christians do when they ignore the "wrath and damnation" stuff. Both sides have Scriptural support for their version of Christianity. And neither side has any better evidence for why the cherries they picked are the ones Jesus wants us to eat. When Christians of any stripe look at other Christians and say, "They're not true Christians," the question I always want to ask is, "How do you know?"

I'll tell you how they know. They don't. When you ask progressive Christians why they believe their Christianity is the true one, all they can ultimately say is, "That's just what I believe," or, "I feel it in my heart." Like all believers, their belief that they're accurately perceiving God's message comes down to the conviction of faith. But the Christian Right has just as much conviction. They feel it in their hearts just as powerfully. Their faith in a pissy, bigoted, judgmental Christ who's obsessed with who's fucking who and how… it's every bit as strong as liberal Christians' faith in a gentle, forgiving Christ who wants us to treat one another with compassion.

And it's not like the Christian Right is some obscure sect that believes Jesus is a space alien or something. They're the largest, most politically powerful religious group in the United States. The hellfire version of Christianity is a huge part of the reality and history of the faith.

This whole "they're not true Christians" thing is what atheists and rationalists call the "no true Scotsman" fallacy. Imagine that Angus McTavish reads about a grisly murder committed in London, and says to himself, "No Scotsman would commit such a terrible crime." Then the next day, he reads about an equally grisly murder committed in Glasgow… and says to himself, "No true Scotsman would commit such a terrible crime." But Angus McTavish doesn't get to decide that a grisly murderer can't be a true Scotsman. And progressive Christians don't get to decide that right-wing fundamentalists can't be true Christians.

By all means, say that the Christian Right is wrong. Say that their vision of the world is hateful and bigoted and out of touch with reality. Say that their version of Christianity isn't the only one, even. I'll stand by you. But don't say that they're not true Christians. They are Christians, by any reasonable definition of the word. You don't have the one true version of the faith, any more than they do.

(Note: The hair dryer analogy comes from "Letter to a Christian Nation" by Sam Harris. The extrapolation of the analogy into "why nice religion is still problematic" belongs to a comment by Brownian at Pharyngula. The "no true Scotsman" analogy was originally developed by Anthony Flew, in his book "Thinking About Thinking: Do I sincerely want to be right?")

CHAPTER FIVE

—— ✹ ——

Yes, This Means You: New Age Religion

"But surely you don't mean New Age religion! You're talking about conventional religion, organized religion, religion with dogma and authority and a power structure. I understand being angry about that. But New Age religion and spirituality doesn't have any of that! It's transcendent, and healing, and fluid, and connected with nature and stuff! When you talk about what makes atheists mad about religion… surely you don't mean me?"

Actually—yes, I do mean you.

It's true that when I write about religion and religious belief, I tend to write about the Big Ones. The famous ones, the powerful ones, the well-organized ones with millions of followers or more. (Christianity, mostly, since as an American, it's the one I'm most familiar with, and the one that's most in my face.)

But it isn't just the power structure of religion that's a problem. It's the spiritual belief itself.

So I want to talk about New Age religion. Or, as it's sometimes called, "woo." Neo-paganism. Wicca. Goddess worship. Astrology. Telepathy. Visualization. Psychic healing. The hodgepodge of Eastern and pre-modern religious beliefs imported into modern America—reincarnation, karma, chakras, shamanism etc.—that have been jumbled together and made palatable to a Western audience. Channeling. Tarot cards. Etc.

And I want to talk about why I have a problem with it.

I said this about progressive religion, and I'll say it here: While I do think woo is harmful, I don't think it's as harmful as mainstream religion. Mostly because it's not as powerful. It's not as widespread, as wealthy, as symbiotically intertwined with governments, as the big religions. There's a difference of degree, and it's significant.

But the fact that it's not *as* harmful doesn't mean it's not harmful at all.

There's an obvious, practical, direct way that woo can do harm. And that's the fact that false premises lead to bad decisions. Woo beliefs are untested and untestable at best; tested and demonstrably false at worst. And basing your life on a false premise is going to lead you to bad decisions. Garbage in, garbage out, as the data processors say. And this shows up most obviously when it comes to medicine.

When I was working as a counselor for a birth control clinic, we had a client who had come in for a cervical cap. I asked her what birth control method she was currently using, and she answered, "Visualization." Really. She and her partner protected themselves from unwanted pregnancy by visualizing a protective barrier of white light over her cervix, shielding it from the sperm. She had decided to switch to the cervical cap, not because she'd decided that visualization was bullshit, but because she was concerned that she unconsciously wanted to get pregnant, and feared that this unconscious desire would make the visualization ineffective. Poke holes in the white light diaphragm, I guess. (Talk about an unfalsifiable hypothesis. If she didn't get pregnant, visualization worked; if she did get pregnant, it's because she wasn't doing it right.)

So that's part of what I'm talking about. If you believe in the visualization method of birth control, you're a lot more likely to get pregnant when you don't want to. If you believe in psychic healing or the manipulation of the chi energy or whatever, you're a lot less likely to seek tested medical help for your injured leg or your cancer or whatever. (And you're more likely to give up on conventional medicine if it takes longer than you want it to, or takes more work and trial and error than you're willing to give it, or is partly effective but not completely.) That's real, practical, physical harm done by woo.

But this principle doesn't just apply to medical woo.

I once worked in an office with cats (no, this isn't a tangent, bear with me), one of whom was pathologically shy and terrified of most people, but had come to trust me and be very attached to me, pretty much to the exclusion of everyone else. When I left that job (I'd been there for several years), I was worried that he would freak out without me, and asked my boss if I could take the cat home with me. Rather than consider the question on its own merits, my boss called an animal psychic… who did a consultation *over the phone*, and told her the cat wanted to stay in the office. My boss explained this to me, as if it had the force of complete authority. As if the psychic's verdict completely and inarguably settled the question.

I'm not saying this was an easy decision to make. It wasn't. I'm saying that it should have been made by me and my boss, who knew the cat and knew the situation. It should not have been made by a pet psychic, who never met any of us in person, and who made the decision over the phone.

(Slight tangent, although it is in fact relevant: If you want to read one of the funniest things ever about telephone animal psychics, read "Friend's Best Man"[1] by Harmon Leon, a.k.a. The Infiltrator, who called several pet psychics and asked them to do readings on his dog… a dog who did not, in fact, exist.)

I could give example after example of this. If you believe that your horoscopes and Tarot readings are all pointing to "serious love relationship coming soon," you're not going to make smart or careful decisions about your dating life. If you believe in reincarnation, you're going to be more careless about taking advantage of once-in-a-lifetime opportunities and experiences and how they're both humbled. If you believe that the Tarot is telling you to weather the rough spots in your relationship and that there's light at the end of the tunnel, you're going to stay in a destructive, hopeless relationship for a lot longer than you should. You might even marry the guy. (All examples from my own life, by the way.)

So that's the most direct, immediate way that woo can do harm. False premises lead to bad decisions. And untestable hypotheses make it impossible to evaluate your decision-making process and adjust it. Garbage in, garbage out.

But there's an equally important way that woo can do harm. And that's that it leads people away from valuing reason, and evidence, and reality. Woo, like every other religious or spiritual belief, ultimately prioritizes faith over reason; personal experience over external evidence.

I'm not saying that religious belief completely eradicates reason or concern for evidence. I'm saying that, when it comes down to a hard choice between the two, it encourages people to reject reason and evidence in favor of personal experience. Religious belief encourages people to believe in their own feelings and instincts... even when those feelings and instincts are contradicted by reality or logic. It discourages people from being aware of the fact that their feelings and instincts can be deceived: by con artists and charlatans, or just by our own wishful thinking. It discourages people from being aware of this well-documented fact, and staying vigilant about it. Every unsupported belief you hold makes you more vulnerable to others... and less likely to value skepticism and critical thinking at all.

I think this is important. I think reality is important. I think reality is just about the most important thing there is. And I have a serious problem with any belief system that encourages people to ignore it. It's hard enough to be vigilant and conscious and skeptical about your biases and blind spots when you do prioritize reason and reality over instinct and personal feeling. Throwing spiritual faith into the mix makes it even harder.

Now, as my wife Ingrid points out when we discuss this, there are some woo believers—neo-pagans and Wiccans especially—who take it all with a grain of salt. There are believers—a better word would be practitioners—who see the ideas more as useful metaphors, and who see the rituals as comforting and beautiful rather than literally effective. They see woo as a way of altering their consciousness, re-wiring their own heads—not as a way of directly changing external reality. And that kind of woo, I don't have a huge problem with.

But I also think it can be a dicey path to walk. I remember, from my own woo days, how vague and half-assed my beliefs could be. And I remember how easily I could slip back and forth between thinking of my beliefs as metaphorical, and thinking of them as literal. Mostly, they slipped back and forth depending on how hard they were being questioned. When I was with someone who was more skeptical, I'd lean toward the "useful metaphor" end of the spectrum: when I was with other believers, I'd lean toward the, "Wow, isn't this freaky, something weird must be going on here!" side. And I know from experience that other woo believers do this as well. A commenter on my blog, John the Drunkard, summarized the attitude beautifully[2]: "We don't really believe anything that you have demonstrated to be absurd… while anyone is watching." When explaining their theology in public, when debating their theology with skeptics, they don't admit to believing anything that contradicts evidence or logic. But in the company of other believers, and in the privacy of their own minds… it's another story.

And if religion really is just a metaphor, then why do people get so upset when atheists say that it isn't true? If religion is simply a story, a personal perspective, a way of framing experience and giving it meaning, then why are people troubled and even angered when someone says, "Actually, that probably isn't true"? Any more than they'd be troubled if someone said, "Actually, *Alice in Wonderland* probably isn't true"? If you're getting upset when people point out that religion isn't true, then I have to question whether you sincerely see it as simply a metaphor. And if you are going with the "this is just powerful metaphor and a useful practice" route, you need to do it consistently and with integrity—and not just as a way of dodging skeptical critiques.

But why do you need to do that? What business is it of mine whether other people's practices are rigorously naturalistic or slip into supernatural belief? Don't people have the right to believe whatever they want to believe?

Of course we have the right to come to our own conclusions about religion. I will defend that right passionately and ferociously. We have the right to believe that a mystical spirit guides the Tarot cards; that subatomic particles have free will; that our romantic lives are guided by balls of flaming gas billions of light years away; that psychics can detect our pets' true desires over the phone; that Jesus Christ is our personal savior and anyone who doesn't agree is going to Hell.

But that doesn't mean it's right for us to do so.

I'm free to believe anything I want. But I can't do so and be honest with myself. I can't do so and retain my intellectual integrity. I can't do so if I'm going to make good decisions based in reality—the best possible understanding of reality we have. I can't do so if I'm going to place reality as more important, and more interesting, than my own wishful thinking. As the saying goes, you have a right to your own beliefs, but you don't have a right to your own facts.

And our beliefs don't just affect our own lives. They affect how we treat other people. My decision to stay in a bad relationship because the Tarot told me to didn't affect only me. My client's decision to prevent pregnancy with wishful thinking didn't affect only her. My boss's decision to consult a pet psychic about our office cat didn't affect only her. (For one thing, she spent money on the psychic at a time when she was having a hard time paying her staff.) And this doesn't just apply to our personal lives: it works on a larger social-justice scale as well. The belief in karma and reincarnation, for instance, gets used to justify terrible social ills, and to treat people born into poverty and despair as if they're simply getting what they deserve. Our beliefs affect our behavior towards others. And that makes our beliefs, not just a personal question, but an ethical one.

If it were possible to believe in woo—not just in a "useful metaphor" way, but to genuinely believe in it—and not make bad decisions, not be held back by sloppy thinking, not be hurt emotionally, not hurt others, not lose reason as the guiding point of your life… then no. I wouldn't have nearly as much of a problem with it.

But I don't think that's possible.

CHAPTER SIX

— ✦ —

Yes, This Means You: "Spiritual but Not Religious"

"But surely you don't mean spirituality! The problem isn't with spirituality—spirituality is what connects us with the greatest things in the Universe! The problem is with organized religion, with following somebody else's ideas about God and the soul. I don't do that! I'm spiritual, but I'm not religious. When you talk about what makes atheists mad about religion… surely you don't mean me?"

Actually—yes, I do mean you.

"Spiritual, but not religious." You've almost certainly heard this trope. It doesn't necessarily mean that the person is New Agey (although it often does). People use it who hold more or less traditional beliefs in a deity, but who've left their organized religion or never belonged to one. (For those people, the trope often goes, "I'm not religious, but I worship God in my own way.") People use it to mean they believe in something other than the physical world: they don't know what exactly, but they're pretty sure it's something. People even use it to mean that they find some sort of meaning and transcendence in life, and don't have another word for that other than "spirituality."

But I don't think disorganized spirituality holds any more water than organized religion. And while "spiritual but not religious" doesn't have the power of traditional religion to brutalize or oppress, it still leads people to derail their critical thinking, and trivialize reality, and prioritize personal bias over evidence, and base important decisions on a foundation of sand.

When I'm in a generous mood, I see this as a valid desire to not be connected with the horrors of organized religion… while still feeling a personal experience that people think is a connection with God. (Or the Goddess, or the spirit world, or whatever.) They're trying to separate the wheat from the chaff. And while I think they're dead wrong about God—I think it's all chaff—I understand the impulse.

And sometimes "spiritual but not religious" is a gateway drug, a baby step out of religious belief. For people who are questioning religion but have been brought up to think it's the source of all morality and meaning, "spiritual but not religious" can help them begin to let go, without feeling like they're stepping into the abyss. And I can definitely be generous about that.

When I'm in a less generous mood, though, I see this trope as smug and superior, without anything to back it up. I see it as a way of saying, "I'm so special and independent, of course I don't have anything to do with hidebound organized religion, I'm far too free a spirit… but I'm also special and sensitive, and in touch with powerful sacred things beyond this mundane world."

So what's my problem with it? Other than the smugness, I mean.

The obvious problem, of course, is that there's not a shred of good evidence to back it up. There's no more evidence for disorganized religion than there is for organized religion.

And "spiritual but not religious" tends to be a sloppy form of spirituality. It lacks even the tortured rigor of carefully thought-out theology; the discipline, pointless though it may be, of fervent religious practice. All too often, "spiritual but not religious" seems to mean, "I believe in some sort of supernatural world, but I'm not willing to give that belief much thought, or to seriously consider whether the spiritual world I believe in makes a lick of sense."

Rather more importantly: I think the "spiritual but not religious" trope plays into the idea that religious belief—excuse me, spiritual belief—makes you a finer, better person. There's a defensiveness to it: like the person is saying, "I don't attend religious services or engage in any religious practice… but I'm not a bad person. Of course I still feel a connection to God and the soul. I haven't completely descended to the gutter. What do you take me for?" It gives aid and comfort to the idea that value and joy, transcendence and meaning, must come from the world of the supernatural.

But my biggest problem with this trope? If being "spiritual but not religious" means rejecting organized religion while supposedly being in touch with sacred things beyond the mundane physical world… it shows a piss-poor attitude towards the mundane physical world.

The physical world is anything but mundane. The physical world is black holes at the center of every spiral galaxy. It is billions of galaxies rushing away from each other at breakneck speed. It is solid matter that's anything but solid: particles that can't be seen by the strongest microscope, separated by gaping vastnesses of nothing. It is living things that are all related, all with the same great-great-great-to the power of a million grandmother. It is space that curves, continents that drift. It is cells of organic tissue that somehow generate consciousness. When you take the time to learn about the mundane physical world, you find that it is anything but mundane.

And this crap about "I don't follow any organized religion, but there has to be more to life than what we see" does a grave disservice to the wild and astonishing complexity of what we see.

As someone whose name I can't remember once wrote: The "spiritual but not religious" trope tries to have the best of both worlds… but it actually gets the worst. It keeps the part of religion that's the indefensible, unsupported-by-a-scrap-of-evidence belief in invisible beings; indeed, the part of religion that sees those invisible beings as more real, and more important, than the physical world we live in. It keeps the part of religion that devalues reason and evidence and critical thinking, in favor of hanging onto any cockamamie idea that appeals to your wishful thinking. It keeps the part of religion that equates morality and value with believing in invisible friends. It keeps the part of religion that confers a smug sense of superiority, solely on the basis of your supposed connection with an invisible world.

It keeps all that… and abandons the part of religion that's community, and shared ritual, and charitable works, and a sense of belonging. It throws out the baby, and keeps the bathwater. And then it pats itself on the back and says, "Look at all this wonderful bathwater I have!"

CHAPTER SEVEN

———✦———

Yes, This Means You: Ecumenicalism and Interfaith

"But surely you don't mean interfaith religion! The problem with traditional religion is how intolerant it is of other religions. But lots of believers aren't like that! We have respect for other people's religions! We want to understand them, and work in peace and harmony with them! When you talk about what makes atheists mad about religion… surely you don't mean me?"

Actually—yes, I do mean you.

Among progressive and moderate religious believers, this ecumenical, interfaith, "Can't we all just get along?" idea is a big deal. For many of these believers, being respectful of religious beliefs that are different from theirs is a central guiding principle. In this view, different religions are seen as a beautifully varied tapestry of faith: each strand with its own truths, each with its own unique perspective on God and its own unique way of worshipping him. Her. It. Them. Whatever. Respecting other people's religious beliefs is a cornerstone of this worldview… to the point where criticizing or even questioning anyone else's belief is seen as rude and offensive at best, bigoted and intolerant at worst.

And this ecumenical approach to religion drives me up a tree.

Why? Don't atheists want a world where everyone's right to their own religious views—including the right to no religious views—is universally acknowledged? Don't we want a world with no religious wars or hatred? Don't we want a world where a diversity of perspectives on religion is accepted and even embraced? Why would atheists have any objection to the principles of interfaith and religious ecumenicalism?

Where shall I begin? Well, for starters: It's bullshit.

Progressive and moderate religious believers absolutely have objections to religious beliefs that are different from theirs. Serious, passionate objections. They object to the Religious Right; they object to Al Qaeda. They object to right-wing fundamentalists preaching homophobic hatred, to Muslim extremists executing women for adultery, to the Catholic Church trying to stop condom distribution for AIDS prevention in Africa, to religious extremists all over the Middle East trying to bomb each other back to the Stone Age. Etc., etc., etc. Even when they share the same nominal faith as these believers, they are appalled at the connection: they fervently reject being seen as having anything in common with them, and often go to great lengths to distance themselves from them.

And they should. I'm not saying they shouldn't. In fact, one of my main critiques of progressive believers is that their opposition to hateful religious extremists often isn't vehement enough.

But it's disingenuous at best, hypocritical at worst, to say that criticism of other religious beliefs is inherently bigoted and offensive… and then make an exception for beliefs that are opposed to your own. You don't get to speak out about how the hard-line extremists are getting Christ's message wrong (or Mohammad's, or Moses', or Buddha's, or whoever)—and then squawk about religious intolerance when others say you're the one getting it wrong. That's not playing fair.

And, of course, it's ridiculously hypocritical to engage in fervent political and cultural discourse—as so many progressive ecumenical believers do—and then expect religion to get a free pass. It's absurd to accept and even welcome vigorous public debate over politics, science, gender, sexuality, medicine, economics, education, the role of government, etc… and then get appalled and insulted when religion is treated as just another hypothesis about the world, one that can be debated and criticized like any other.

However, if ecumenicalism were just hypocrisy, I wouldn't care that much. Hypocrisy is all over the human race like a cheap suit. I'm not going to get worked up into a lather every time I see another example of it. So why does this bug me so much?

Well, it also bugs me because—in an irony that would be hilarious if it weren't so screwed-up—a commitment to ecumenicalism all too often leads to intolerance and hostility towards atheists.

I've been in a lot of debates with religious believers over the years. And some of the ugliest, nastiest, most bigoted anti-atheist rhetoric I've heard has come from progressive and moderate believers espousing the supposedly tolerant principles of ecumenicalism. I've been called a fascist, a zealot, a missionary; I've been called hateful, intolerant, close-minded, dogmatic; I've had my atheist activism described as "cultural imperialism" and equated with the genocide of the Native Americans[1]; I've been compared to Glenn Beck and Joseph Stalin and Adolph Hitler. All by progressive and moderate believers, outraged at the very notion of atheists pointing out the flaws in religious ideas and making an argument that these ideas are probably not true. Progressive and moderate believers who normally are passionate advocates for free expression will get equally passionate about demanding that atheists shut the hell up. Progressive and moderate believers who normally are all over the idea of diversity and multi-culturalism will get intensely defensive of homogeny when one of the voices in the rich cultural tapestry is saying, "I don't think God exists, and here's why."

In a way, I can see it. Ecumenicalism is a big, comfy love-fest. (Or, to use a less polite metaphor, a big, happy circle-jerk.) Everyone stands around telling each other how wonderful they are, how fascinating their viewpoint is, how much they contribute to humanity's rich and evolving vision of God. Everyone is self-deprecating about how their own vision of God is human and flawed and limited, and how they're both humbled and uplifted to see such different perspectives on him/her/it/them/whatever. Everyone tells the story of the six blind men and the elephant, and how God is too vast and complex and unfathomable for any one person to perfectly understand him, and how all these different religions are just perceiving different aspects of his immensity. And no one ever says anything critical, or even seriously questioning. It's one gigantic mutual admiration society.

And then atheists come along, and ruin everyone's party. Atheists come along and say, "We don't think any of you are getting it right." Atheists come along and ask hard questions, like, "You have important differences between your religions—how do you decide which one is true?" Or, "Religion has never once in all of human history turned out to be the right answer to any question—why would you think it's the right answer to anything we don't currently understand?" Or, "If there's no way your belief can be proven wrong, how do you know that it's right?" Or, "Why do the six blind men just give up? Why don't they compare notes and trade places and carefully examine the elephant to try to figure out what it is? You know—the way we do in science? Why doesn't this work with religion? Sure, if God existed, he/she/it/they would be vast and complex and hard to fathom… and what, the physical Universe isn't? Doesn't the fact that this never, ever works with religion strongly suggest that it's all made up, and there is, in fact, no elephant?" Atheists come along and make unnerving points like, "The fact that you can't come to any consensus about religion isn't a point in your favor—in fact, it's one of the strongest points against you." Atheists come along, like the rain god on everyone's parade, and say things like, "What reason do any you have to think any of this is true?"

No wonder they don't like us.

Which leads me to the final objection I have to religious ecumenicalism, and by far the most important one:

It shows a callous disregard for the truth.

This idea that religion is just a matter of opinion? That the most crucial questions about how the Universe works and how it came into being should be set aside, because disagreements about it might upset people? That it doesn't matter who has the correct understanding of God or the soul or whatever, and when faced with different ideas about these questions, it's best to just shrug it off, and agree to disagree, and go on thinking whatever makes us feel good? That figuring out what probably is and is not true about the world is a lower priority than not hurting anyone's feelings? That reality is less important, and less interesting, than the stories people make up about it?

It drives me up a tree.

In my debates and discussions with religious believers, there's a question that I've asked many times: "Do you care whether the things you believe are true?" And I'm shocked at how many times I've gotten the answer, "No, not really." It leaves me baffled, practically speechless. (Hey, I said "practically.") I mean, even leaving out the pragmatic failure and the moral and philosophical bankruptcy of prioritizing pleasantry over reality... isn't it disrespectful to the god you supposedly believe in? If you genuinely loved God, wouldn't you want to understand him as best you can? When faced with different ideas about God, wouldn't you want to ask some questions, and look at the supporting evidence for the different views, and try to figure out which one is probably true? Doesn't it seem insulting to God to treat that question as if it didn't matter?

There are profound differences between religions. They are not trivial. And the different religions cannot all be right. (Although, as atheists like to point out, they can all be wrong.) Jesus cannot both be and not be the son of God. God cannot be both an intentional, sentient being and a diffuse supernatural force animating all life. God cannot be both a personal intervening force in our daily lives and a vague metaphorical abstraction of the concepts of love and existence. Dead people cannot both go to Heaven and be reincarnated. Etc. Etc. Etc.

When faced with these different ideas, are you seriously going to shrug your shoulders, and say "My, how fascinating, look at all these different ideas, isn't it amazing how many ways people have of seeing God, what a magnificent tapestry of faith humanity has created"?

Do you really not care which of these ideas is, you know, true?

A part of me can see where the ecumenicalists are coming from. I think they look at a history filled with religious war and hatred, bigotry and violence… and they recoil in horror and revulsion. And they should. I recoil from that stuff, too. It's not why I'm an atheist—I'm an atheist because I think the religion hypothesis is implausible and unsupported by any good evidence—but it's a big part of why I'm an atheist activist. Heck—it's the main reason I wrote this book.

But the ecumenicalists seem to think there are only two options for dealing with religious differences: (a) intolerant evangelism and theocracy, in which people with different religious views are shunned at best and outlawed or brutalized at worst… or (b) uncritical interfaith ecumenicalism, in which differences between religious views are ignored whenever possible, and handled with kid gloves when some sort of handling is necessary. Ecumenicalists eagerly embrace the second option, largely in horrified response to the first… and they tend to treat any criticism of any religion as if it were automatically part of that ugly, bigoted, violent history.

They don't see that there's a third option.

They don't see that there's an option of respecting the important freedom of religious belief… while retaining the right to criticize those beliefs, and to treat them just like we'd treat any other idea we think is mistaken. They don't see the option of being passionate about the right to religious freedom, of fully supporting the right to come to our own conclusions about religion as one of our fundamental human rights…

while at the same time seeing the right to criticize ideas we don't agree with as an equally fundamental right. They don't see the option of debating and disagreeing without resorting to hatred and violence. They don't see the option of disagreeing with what people say, while defending to the death their right to say it.

You know. The option advocated by most atheist activists.

I will say this: If the only religious believers in the world were progressive and moderate ecumenical ones, most atheists wouldn't care very much. We'd still disagree with religion; we'd still think it was implausible at best and ridiculous at worst. But it wouldn't get up our noses that much. We'd see it about the same way we see, say, urban legends, or those Internet forwards your aunt Tilda keeps sending you: kind of silly, mildly annoying, but mostly harmless, and not worth getting worked up about. (And, in fact, while I disagree pretty strongly with ecumenical believers, I'm happy to share a world with them, to work in alliance with them on issues we have in common, to sit down at the dinner table with them and enjoy a long evening of food and booze and conversation. As long as we don't talk about religion.)

But ecumenicalists are not the only believers. Not by a long shot. When it comes to religion, "live and let live" believers are very much in the minority. And progressive and moderate religion lends an unfortunate credibility to the conservative and extreme varieties. It lends credibility to the idea that faith is more valuable than evidence; to the idea that it's reasonable to believe things we have no good reason to think are true; to the idea that wishful thinking is a good enough reason to believe something. It lends credibility to all the things about religion that makes it most uniquely harmful.

And this ecumenical attitude that reality is an annoying distraction from the far more important business of feeling good—and that insisting on reality is an ugly form of bigoted intolerance—is part and parcel of this unique armor that religion has built against valid criticism, questioning, and self-correction.

It is not a protection against the evils of religion.

It is one of them.

CHAPTER EIGHT

———— ✸ ————

The Top Ten Reasons I Don't Believe In God

"But just because religion has done some harm—that doesn't mean it's mistaken! Sure, people have done terrible things in God's name. That doesn't mean God doesn't exist!"

Yup. If you're arguing that—you're absolutely right. And the question of whether religion is true or not is important. It's not the main point of this book: if you want more thorough arguments for why God doesn't exist, by me or other writers, check out the Resource Guide at the end of this book. But "Does God exist?" is a valid and relevant question. Here are my Top Ten reasons why the answer is a resounding, "No."

1: The consistent replacement of supernatural explanations of the world with natural ones. When you look at the history of what we know about the world, you see a noticeable pattern. Natural explanations of things have been replacing supernatural explanations of them. Like a steamroller. Why the Sun rises and sets. Where thunder and lightning come from. Why people get sick. Why people look like their parents. How the complexity of life came into being. I could go on and on.

All these things were once explained by religion. But as we understood the world better, and learned to observe it more carefully, the

95

explanations based on religion were replaced by ones based on physical cause and effect. Consistently. Thoroughly. Like a steamroller. The number of times that a supernatural explanation of a phenomenon has been replaced by a natural explanation? Thousands upon thousands upon thousands.

Now. The number of times that a natural explanation of a phenomenon has been replaced by a supernatural one? The number of times humankind has said, "We used to think (X) was caused by physical cause and effect, but now we understand that it's caused by God, or spirits, or demons, or the soul"?

Exactly zero.

Sure, people come up with new supernatural "explanations" for stuff all the time. But explanations with evidence? Replicable evidence? Carefully gathered, patiently tested, rigorously reviewed evidence? Internally consistent evidence? Large amounts of it, from many different sources? Again—exactly zero.

Given that this is true, what are the chances that any given phenomenon for which we currently don't have a thorough explanation—human consciousness, for instance, or the origin of the Universe—will be best explained by the supernatural?

Given this pattern, it's clear that the chances of this are essentially zero. So close to zero that they might as well be zero. And the hypothesis of the supernatural is therefore a hypothesis we can discard. It is a hypothesis we came up with when we didn't understand the world as well as we do now... but that, on more careful examination, has never once been shown to be correct.

If I see any solid evidence to support God, or any supernatural explanation of any phenomenon, I'll reconsider my disbelief. Until then, I'll assume that the mind-bogglingly consistent pattern of natural explanations replacing supernatural ones is almost certain to continue.

(Oh—for the sake of brevity, I'm generally going to say "God" in this chapter when I mean "God, or the soul, or metaphysical energy, or any sort of supernatural being or substance." I don't feel like getting into discussions about, "Well, I don't believe in an old man in the clouds with a white beard, but I believe…" It's not just the man in the white beard that I don't believe in. I don't believe in *any* sort of religion, *any* sort of soul or spirit or metaphysical guiding force, *anything* that isn't the physical world and its vast and astonishing manifestations.)

2: The inconsistency of world religions. If God (or any other metaphysical being or beings) were real, and people were really perceiving him/her/it/them, why do these perceptions differ so wildly?

When different people look at, say, a tree, we more or less agree about what we're looking at: what size it is, what shape, whether it currently has leaves or not and what color those leaves are, etc. We may have disagreements regarding the tree—what other plants it's most closely related to, where it stands in the evolutionary scheme, should it be cut down to make way for a new sports stadium, etc. But unless one of us is hallucinating or deranged or literally unable to see, we can all agree on the tree's basic existence, and the basic facts about it.

This is blatantly not the case for God. Even among people who do believe in God, there is no agreement about what God is, what God does, what God wants from us, how he acts or doesn't act on the world, whether he's a he, whether there's one or more of him, whether he's a personal being or a diffuse metaphysical substance. And this is among smart, thoughtful people. What's more, many smart, thoughtful people don't even think God exists.

And if God existed, he'd be a whole lot bigger, a whole lot more powerful, with a whole lot more effect in the world, than a tree. Why is it that we can all see a tree in more or less the same way, but we don't see God in even remotely the same way?

The explanation, of course, is that God does not exist. We disagree so radically over what he is because we aren't perceiving anything that's real. We're "perceiving" something we made up; something we were taught to believe; something that the part of our brain that's wired to see pattern and intention, even when none exists, is inclined to see and believe.

3: The weakness of religious arguments, explanations, and apologetics. I have seen a lot of arguments for the existence of God. And they all boil down to one or more of the following: The argument from authority. (Example: "God exists because the Bible says God exists.") The argument from personal experience. (Example: "God exists because I feel in my heart that God exists.") The argument that religion shouldn't have to logically defend its claims. (Example: "God is an entity that cannot be proven by reason or evidence.") Or the redefining of God into an abstract principle... so abstract that it can't be argued against, but also so abstract that it scarcely deserves the name God. (Example: "God is love.")

And all these arguments are ridiculously weak.

Sacred books and authorities can be mistaken. I have yet to see a sacred book that doesn't have any mistakes. (The Bible, to give just one example, is shot full of them[1].) And the feelings in people's hearts can definitely be mistaken. They are mistaken, demonstrably so, much of the time. Instinct and intuition play an important part in human understanding and experience... but they should never be treated as the final word on a subject. I mean, if I told you, "The tree in front of my house is 500 feet tall with hot pink leaves," and I offered as a defense, "I know this is true because my mother/preacher/sacred book tells me so"... or "I know this is true because I feel it in my heart"... would you take me seriously?

Some people do try to prove God's existence by pointing to evidence in the world. But that evidence is inevitably terrible. Pointing to the perfection of the Bible as a historical and prophetic document, for instance... when it so blatantly is nothing of the kind.[2] Or pointing to the fine-tuning of the Universe for life... even though this supposedly perfect fine-tuning is actually pretty crappy, and the conditions that allow for life on Earth have only existed for the tiniest fragment of the Universe's existence and are going to be boiled away by the Sun in about a billion years.[3] Or pointing to the complexity of life and the world and insisting that it must have been designed… when the sciences of biology and geology and such have provided far, far better explanations for what seems, at first glance, like design.[4]

As to the argument that "We don't have to show you any reason or evidence, it's unreasonable and intolerant for you to even expect that"… that's conceding the game before you've even begun. It's like saying, "I know I can't make my case—therefore I'm going to concentrate my arguments on why I don't have to make my case in the first place." It's like a defense lawyer who knows their client is guilty, so they try to get the case thrown out on a technicality.

Ditto with the "redefining God out of existence" argument. If what you believe in isn't a supernatural being or substance that has, or at one time had, some sort of effect on the world… well, your philosophy might be an interesting one, but it is not, by any useful definition of the word, religion.

Again: If I tried to argue, "The tree in front of my house is 500 feet tall with hot pink leaves—and the height and color of trees is a question that is best answered with personal faith and feeling, not with reason or evidence"… or, "I know this is true because I am defining '500 feet tall and hot pink' as the essential nature of tree-ness, regardless of its outward appearance"… would you take me seriously?

4: The increasing diminishment of God. This is closely related to #1 (the consistent replacement of supernatural explanations of the world with natural ones). But it's different enough to deserve its own section.

When you look at the history of religion, you see that the perceived power of God has been diminishing. As our understanding of the physical world has increased—and as our ability to test theories and claims has improved—the domain of God's miracles and interventions, or other supposed supernatural phenomena, has consistently shrunk.

Examples: We stopped needing God to explain floods... but we still needed him to explain sickness and health. Then we didn't need him to explain sickness and health... but we still needed him to explain consciousness. Now we're beginning to get a grip on consciousness, so we'll soon need God to explain... what?

Or, as writer and blogger Adam Lee so eloquently put it in his Ebon Musings website, "Where the Bible tells us God once shaped worlds out of the void and parted great seas with the power of his word, today his most impressive acts seem to be shaping sticky buns into the likenesses of saints and conferring vaguely-defined warm feelings on his believers' hearts when they attend church."[5]

This is what atheists call the "god of the gaps." Whatever gap there is in our understanding of the world, that's what God is supposedly responsible for. Wherever the empty spaces are in our coloring book, that's what gets filled in with the blue crayon called God.

But the blue crayon is worn down to a nub. And it's never turned out to be the right color. And over and over again, throughout history, we've had to go to great trouble to scrape the blue crayon out of people's minds and replace it with the right color. Given this pattern, doesn't it seem that we should stop reaching for the blue crayon every time we see an empty space in the coloring book?

5: The fact that religion runs in families. The single strongest factor in determining what religion a person is? It's what religion they were brought up with. By far. Very few people carefully examine all the available religious beliefs—or even some of those beliefs—and select the one they think most accurately describes the world. Overwhelmingly, people believe whatever religion they were taught as children.[6]

Now, we don't do this with, for instance, science. We don't hold on to the Steady State theory of the Universe, or geocentrism, or the four bodily humours theory of illness, simply because it's what we were taught as children. We believe whatever scientific understanding is best supported by the best available evidence at the time. And if the evidence changes, our understanding changes. (Unless, of course, it's a scientific understanding that our religion teaches is wrong…)

Even political opinions don't run in families as stubbornly as religion. Witness the opinion polls that show support of same-sex marriage increasing with each new generation.[7] Political beliefs learned from youth can, and do, break down in the face of the reality that people see every day. And scientific theories do this, all the time, on a regular basis.

This is emphatically not the case with religion.

Which leads me to the conclusion that religion is not a perception of a real entity. If it were, people wouldn't just believe whatever religion they were taught as children, simply because it was what they were taught as children. The fact that religion runs so firmly in families strongly suggests that it is not a perception of a real phenomenon. It is a dogma, supported and perpetuated by tradition and social pressure—and in many cases, by fear and intimidation. Not by reality.

6: The physical causes of everything we think of as the soul. The sciences of neurology and neuropsychology are in their infancy. But they are advancing by astonishing leaps and bounds, even as we speak. And what they are finding—consistently, thoroughly, across the board—is that, whatever consciousness is, it is inextricably linked to the brain.

Everything we think of as the soul—consciousness, identity, character, free will—all of that is powerfully affected by physical changes to the brain and body. Changes in the brain result in changes in consciousness… sometimes so drastically, they make a personality unrecognizable. Changes in consciousness can be seen, with magnetic resonance imagery, as changes in the brain. Illness, injury, drugs and medicines, sleep deprivation, etc…. all of these can make changes to the supposed "soul," both subtle and dramatic. And death, of course, is a physical change that renders a person's personality and character, not only unrecognizable, but non-existent.

So the obvious conclusion is that consciousness and identity, character and free will, are products of the brain and the body. They're biological processes, governed by laws of physical cause and effect. With any other phenomenon, if we can show that physical forces and actions produce observable effects, we think of that as a physical phenomenon. Why should the "soul" be any different?

What's more, the evidence supporting this conclusion comes from rigorously-gathered, carefully-tested, thoroughly cross-checked, double-blinded, placebo-controlled, replicated, peer-reviewed research. The evidence has been gathered, and continues to be gathered, using the gold standard of scientific evidence: methods specifically designed to filter out biases and cognitive errors as much as humanly possible. And it's not just a little research. It's an enormous mountain of research… a mountain that's growing more mountainous every day.

The hypothesis of the soul, on the other hand, has not once in all of human history been supported by good, solid scientific evidence. That's pretty surprising when you think about it. For decades, and indeed centuries, most scientists had some sort of religious beliefs, and most of them believed in the soul. So a great deal of early science was dedicated to proving the soul's existence, and discovering and exploring its nature. It wasn't until after decades upon decades of fruitless research in this area that scientists finally gave it up as a bad job, and concluded, almost unanimously, that the reason they hadn't found a soul was that there was no such thing.

Are there unanswered questions about consciousness? Absolutely. Tons of them. No reputable neurologist or neuropsychologist would say otherwise. But think again about how the history of human knowledge is the history of supernatural explanations being replaced by natural ones… with relentless consistency, again, and again, and again.

There hasn't been a single exception to this pattern. Why would we assume that the soul is going to be that exception? Why would we assume that this gap in our knowledge, alone among all the others, is eventually going to be filled with a supernatural explanation? The historical pattern doesn't support it. And the evidence doesn't support it. The increasingly clear conclusion of the science is that consciousness is a product of the brain. Period.

7: The complete failure of any sort of supernatural phenomenon to stand up to rigorous testing. Not all religious and spiritual beliefs make testable claims. But some of them do. And in the face of actual testing, every one of those claims falls apart like Kleenex in a hurricane.

Whether it's the power of prayer, or faith healing, or astrology, or life after death: the same pattern is seen. Whenever religious and supernatural beliefs have made testable claims, and those claims have been tested—not half-assedly tested, but really tested, using careful, rigorous, double-blind, placebo-controlled, replicated, etc. etc. etc. testing methods—the claims have consistently fallen apart. Occasionally a scientific study has appeared that claimed to support something supernatural… but more thorough studies have always refuted them. Every time.

I'm not going to cite each one of these tests, or even most of them. This chapter is already long as it is. Instead, I'll encourage you to spend a little time on the Committee for Skeptical Inquiry and Skeptical Inquirer websites. You'll see a pattern so consistent it boggles the mind: Claimants insist that Supernatural Claim X is real. Supernatural Claim X is subjected to careful testing, applying the standard scientific methods used in research to screen out bias and fraud. Supernatural Claim X is found to hold about as much water as a sieve. (And claimants, having agreed beforehand that the testing method is valid, afterwards insist that it wasn't fair.)

And don't say, "Oh, the testers were biased." That's the great thing about the scientific method. It's designed to screen out bias, as much as is humanly possible. When done right, it will give you the right answer, regardless of the bias of the people doing the testing.

And I want to repeat an important point about the supposed anti-religion bias in science. In the early days of science and the scientific method, most scientists did believe in God, and the soul, and the metaphysical. In fact, many early science experiments were attempts to prove the existence of these things, and discover their true natures, and resolve the squabbles about them once and for all. It was only after decades of these experiments failing to turn up anything at all that the scientific community began—gradually, and very reluctantly—to give up on the idea.

Supernatural claims only hold up under careless, casual examination. They are supported by wishful thinking, and confirmation bias (i.e., our tendency to overemphasize evidence that supports what we believe and to discard evidence that contradicts it), and our poor understanding and instincts when it comes to probability, and our tendency to see pattern and intention even when none exists, and a dozen other forms of cognitive bias and weird human brain wiring. When studied carefully, under conditions specifically designed to screen these things out, the claims vanish like the insubstantial imaginings they are.

8: The slipperiness of religious and spiritual beliefs. Not all religious and spiritual beliefs make testable claims. Many of them have a more "saved if we do, saved if we don't" quality. If things go the believer's way, it's a sign of God's grace and intervention; if they don't, then God moves in mysterious ways, and maybe he has a lesson to teach that we don't understand, and it's not up to us to question his will. No matter what happens, it can be twisted to prove that the belief is right.

That is a sure sign of a bad argument.

Here's the thing. It is a well-established principle in the philosophy of science that, if a theory can be supported no matter what possible evidence comes down the pike, it is useless. It has no power to explain what's already happened, or to predict what will happen in the future. The theory of gravity, for instance, could be disproven by things suddenly falling up; the theory of evolution could be disproven by finding rabbits in the pre-Cambrian fossil layer. These theories predict that those things won't happen; if they do, the theories go poof. But if your theory of God's existence holds up no matter what happens—whether your friend with cancer gets better or dies, whether natural disasters strike big sinful cities or small God-fearing towns—then it's a useless theory, with no power to predict or explain anything.

What's more, when atheists challenge theists on their beliefs, the theists' arguments shift and slip around in an annoying "moving the goalposts" way. Hard-line fundamentalists, for instance, will insist on the unchangeable perfect truth of the Bible; but when challenged on its specific historical or scientific errors, they insist that you're not interpreting those passages correctly. (If the book needs interpreting, then how perfect can it be?)

And progressive ecumenical believers can be unbelievably slippery about what they do and don't believe. Is God real, or a metaphor? Does God intervene in the world, or doesn't he? Do they even believe in God, or do they just choose to act as if they believe because they find it useful? Debating with a progressive believer is like wrestling with a fish: the arguments aren't very powerful, but they're slippery, and they don't give you anything firm to grab onto.

Once again, that's a sure sign of a bad argument. If you can't make your case and then stick by it, or modify it, or let it go… then you don't have a good case. (And if you're making any version of the "Shut up, that's why" argument—arguing that it's intolerant to question religious beliefs, or that letting go of doubts about faith makes you a better person, or that doubting faith will get you tortured in Hell, or any of the other classic arguments intended to quash debate rather than address it—that's a sure sign that your argument is in the toilet.)

9: The failure of religion to improve or clarify over time. Over the years and decades and centuries, our understanding of the physical world has grown and clarified by a ridiculous amount. We understand things about the Universe that we couldn't have imagined a thousand years ago, or a hundred, or even ten. Things that make your mouth gape with astonishment just to think about.

And the reason for this is that we came up with an incredibly good method for sorting out good ideas from bad ones. We came up with the scientific method, a self-correcting method for understanding the physical world: a method which—over time, and with the many fits and starts that accompany any human endeavor—has done an astonishingly good job of helping us perceive and understand the world, predict it and shape it, in ways we couldn't have imagined in decades and centuries past. And the scientific method itself is self-correcting. Not only has our understanding of the natural world improved dramatically: our method for understanding it is improving as well.

Our understanding of the supernatural world? Not so much.

Our understanding of the supernatural world is in the same place it's always been: hundreds and indeed thousands of sects, squabbling over which sacred texts and spiritual intuitions are the right ones. We haven't come to any consensus about which religion best understands the supernatural world. We haven't even come up with a method for making that decision. All anyone can do is point to their own sacred text and their own spiritual intuition. And around in the squabbling circle we go.

All of which points to religion, not as a perception of a real being or substance, but as an idea we made up and are clinging to. If religion were a perception of a real being or substance, our understanding of it would be sharpening, clarifying, being refined. We'd have better prayer techniques, more accurate prophecies, something. Anything but people squabbling with greater or lesser degrees of rancor, and nothing to back up their belief.

10: The complete lack of solid evidence for God's existence. This is probably the best argument I have against God's existence: There's no evidence for it. No good evidence, anyway. No evidence that doesn't just amount to opinion and tradition and confirmation bias and all the other stuff I've been talking about. No evidence that doesn't fall apart upon close examination.

And in a perfect world, that should have been the only argument I needed. In a perfect world, I shouldn't have had to spend a month and a half collating and summarizing the reasons I don't believe in God, any more than I would have for Zeus or Quetzalcoatl or the Flying Spaghetti Monster. As thousands of atheists before me have pointed out: It is not up to us to prove that God does not exist. It is up to theists to prove that he does.

In a comment on my blog, arensb made a point on this topic that was so insightful, I'm still smacking myself on the head for not having thought of it myself. I was writing about how believers get upset at atheists when we reject religion after hearing 876,363 bad arguments for it, and how believers react to this by saying, "But you haven't considered Argument #876,364! How can you be so close-minded?" And arensb said:[8]

"If, in fact, it turns out that argument #876,364 is the one that will convince you, WTF didn't the apologists put it in the top 10?"

Why, indeed?

If there's an argument for religion that's convincing—actually convincing, convincing by means of something other than authority, tradition, personal intuition, confirmation bias, fear and intimidation, wishful thinking, or some combination of the above—wouldn't we all know about it?

Wouldn't it have spread like wildfire? Wouldn't it be the Meme of All Memes? I mean, we all saw that Simon's Cat video[9] within about two weeks of it hitting the Internet. Don't you think that the Truly Excellent Argument for God's Existence would have spread even faster, and wider, than some silly cartoon cat video?

If the arguments for religion are so wonderful, why are they so unconvincing to anyone who doesn't already believe?

And why does God need arguments, anyway? Why does God need people to make his arguments for him? Why can't he just reveal his true self, clearly and unequivocally, and settle the question once and for all? If God existed, why wouldn't it just be obvious?

It is not up to atheists to prove that God does not exist. It is up to believers to prove that he does. And in the absence of any good, solid evidence or arguments in favor of God's existence—and in the presence of a whole lot of solid arguments against it—I will continue to be an atheist. God almost certainly does not exist, and it's completely reasonable to act as if he doesn't.

CHAPTER NINE

---✦---

Why "Religion Is Useful" Is a Terrible Argument— The Santa Delusion

"But religion is useful. It makes people happy. It comforts people in hard times. It makes people better-behaved. And losing religious faith can be traumatic. So what difference does it make if it isn't true? Shouldn't we be perpetuating it anyway—or at least leaving it alone? Why do you want to persuade people out of it?"

Atheists hear this a lot. The argument from utility—the defense of religion, not because it's true, but because it's psychologically or socially useful—is freakishly common. If you spend any time reading debates in atheist blogs or forums, you're bound to see it come up.

Now, when atheists hear this "But religion is useful!" argument, our usual response is to say, "Is not!" We point out that countries with high rates of atheism also have high rates of happiness, ethics, and social functioning.[1] (This doesn't prove that atheism causes high social functioning, of course—it's probably the other way around—but it does show that high social functioning can flourish without religion.) We'll point out the many religious believers who cheat, steal, murder, and generally behave very badly… undercutting the notion that religion provides a solid foundation for moral behavior. And we'll point to ourselves, and to other atheists we know, as the most obvious examples of why this notion is bunk: examples of people who don't need religion, who live happy, ethical lives without religion, who in many cases are happier and better without religion.

These are all fair points. I've made them myself. But there's a basic problem with all of them:

They make the argument from utility seem valid.

And I don't want to do that. I think the argument from utility is absurd on the face of it. I think the entire idea of deciding what we think is true based on what we want to be true is laughable. Or it would be, if it weren't so appalling. I've seen this argument advanced many times… and it still shocks me to see otherwise intelligent, thoughtful adults making it. It is preposterous.

So I want to dismantle the entire premise of the argument from utility. I want to dismantle the entire premise that it's reasonable, and even a positive good, to believe in something you have no good reason to think is true… simply because it makes you happy.

The Santa Delusion

Let's draw an analogy. Let's look at another dearly treasured, deeply held belief about how the world works.

Let's look at Santa Claus.

Millions of children are made happy by their belief in Santa. They have fun imagining the presents he's going to bring them. They like visiting him in the department store. They enjoy hearing stories about him, singing songs about him, drawing pictures of him. They get a thrill from putting cookies and cocoa out for him by the fireplace (or the gas heater, or whatever), and seeing them gone the next day. They get more and more excited as Christmas gets closer and the day of his visitation approaches.

What's more, millions of children behave better because they believe in Santa. The desire for great presents, the fear of getting coal in their stockings instead of presents… this has probably resulted in thousands of cleaned rooms, thousands of finished homework assignments, thousands of un-punched siblings. At least during the month of December.

And millions of children get upset when they discover that Santa isn't real. Letting go of Santa can be a distressing experience, one that people remember into adulthood. (This isn't universally true—I was excited to discover that Santa wasn't real, since I figured it out on my own and it made me feel clever and grown-up to have outwitted the adults—but it's not uncommon.)

Would you therefore argue that we ought to believe in Santa?

Would you argue that, because belief in Santa makes children happy and better-behaved, we therefore ought to perpetuate it? Would you argue that, because relinquishing that belief can be upsetting, we ought to go to great lengths to protect children from discovering that Santa isn't real... not only during their childhood, but throughout their adult lives? Would you attend churches and temples of Santa, and leave cookies and cocoa on their red-and-white-plush altars? Would you pity people who don't believe in Santa as joyless and imprisoned in rationality... and would you chastise these a-Santa-ists as intolerant, bigoted proselytizers when they tried to persuade others that Santa wasn't real?

Or would you, instead, think that people ought to grow up? Would you think that, for people who grew up believing in Santa, letting go of that belief is an essential part of becoming an adult? Would you think that we need to understand reality, so we know how to behave in it? Would you think that, in order to make good decisions and function effectively in the world, we need to have the most accurate understanding of it that we can muster... and that if the best evidence suggests that Santa isn't real, we ought to accept that conclusion? Would you look at this idea that we should decide what's true based on what we want to be true, and call it laughable, appalling, absurd on the face of it?

And if you wouldn't argue that belief in Santa is valid simply because it's useful... why would you argue it about God?

Now. You might say that belief in God makes more sense than belief in Santa. You might say that, while we know Santa is a fictional character, the existence of God is, at the very least, an open question… and that therefore, belief in God is more defensible than belief in Santa.

But then you're back to arguing that God is real. Or at least plausible. You've abandoned the argument from utility (which you should, it's a terrible argument), and you've circled back to debating whether God exists, and whether good evidence supports that hypothesis.

And the *whole freaking point* of the argument from utility is that it abandons the case for God being real. The whole point is that it doesn't matter whether God is real… as long as belief in God makes people happy. So you don't get to shore up that argument by saying that God might be real after all. Not unless you're willing to make a convincing case for God being real.

But if you had a convincing case for God being real… why on Earth would you be arguing that it doesn't matter whether he's real, as long as belief in him makes people happy? If you can make a better case for God than you can for Santa… why aren't you making it? Why are you falling back on this absurd notion that grown-ups should believe whatever makes them feel good, regardless of whether that belief has any connection with reality?

And if you think that educated people can handle the reality of a godless world, but the ordinary masses can't—then shame on you. That's not simply untrue. It's patronizing. It's classist and insulting. I urge you to spend some time on the excellent Blue Collar Atheist blog by Hank Fox[2], which will disabuse you of this notion in a hurry. I urge you to read the brilliant piece by Adam Lee on the Daylight Atheism blog about atheist janitors.[3] And in particular, I urge you to read the comments on that piece from atheist janitors themselves, who have plenty of meaning and happiness without religion, who accept and indeed treasure a world with neither Santa nor God—and who resent being treated like the uneducated, unwashed hoi polloi who need to be protected from reality by people who consider themselves their intellectual betters.

The Argument That Eats Itself

Whenever I hear the argument from utility, I consider it a victory for my side. It's a self-defeating argument, an argument that admits it's wrong in the very stating of it. When people start defending the utility of their beliefs regardless of whether they're true, they've conceded. They're essentially saying, "You're right. The things I believe almost certainly aren't true. I can't make a good case for why they're true. Now will you leave me alone and let me believe them anyway?"

Well, if you want to believe things that you know aren't true, you're free to do that. I'm not sure what definition of the word "believe" you're using there… but sure. If for you, "believing" in God means "telling yourself over and over that God exists, in hopes that you can make yourself really think it"… then knock yourself out.

But if that's what you think, then why are you bothering to argue with atheists? If you really just believe things because you want them to be true, why do you care what anyone else thinks?

I'm going to give you the benefit of the doubt. I'm going to assume that you're debating atheists because you want to test your beliefs against the people who will question them the hardest. I'm going to assume that you do, in fact, care whether the things you believe are true.

And I'm going to show the argument from utility for what it is: a last-ditch effort to hang onto a belief that you know isn't supportable, but that you're having a hard time letting go of. I know that religion is hard to let go of: I know that people have emotional attachments, psychological attachments, social attachments, to believing in God, the soul, the supernatural, the afterlife. I've been there. I get it.

So I'm going to give you the respect of treating you like an adult. I'm going to give you the respect of assuming that you're mature enough to face realities that, at first, are hard to face. And I'm going to give you the respect of being straight with you: If you're making the argument from utility, if you're arguing in favor of wishful thinking, you're not living up to your adulthood.

I will tell you that life without religion can be good. Great, even. I'll tell you that life without religion can be liberating, that it can give you a profound sense of connection with humanity and the Universe. I'll tell you that atheists have meaning in our lives, and joy, and comfort in the face of hard times, and solace in the face of death, and a passion to do right. I'll tell you that atheism can be a safe place to land, and that, as the atheist community grows bigger and stronger, it's becoming a safer place every day. I'll tell you that most former believers I know are tickled pink to have let go of their beliefs.

I'm sincere about all of that. But it isn't what's most important. What's most important about atheism is that it's almost certainly true.

And if you're defending religion because it's useful, regardless of whether it's true… then on some level, you know that.

Come on in. The water's fine.

(Note: The core analogy here about Santa was swiped from "Red Neck, Blue Collar, Atheist" by Hank Fox. I'm an ethical atheist, and I believe in giving credit where credit is due.)

CHAPTER TEN

What Do You Want, Anyway?
One Atheist's Mission Statement

"So what do you want, anyway?"

You get it now. Atheists are angry about religion. We think religion is a mistaken idea, and we think it does significantly more harm than good. So what do we want to do about it? Or rather, since I still don't presume to speak for all atheists: What do I want to do about it? Why do I blog so much about atheism? Why do I fly around the country speaking about it? Why did I write this book? When it comes to religion and the lack thereof… what kind of world do I want to see?

I think atheists need to think about this. Otherwise, we're just arguing for the sake of arguing, a mental exercise done at the expense of annoying people. And we have to decide what kind of world we're trying to create, so we know what to do to create it.

I have a couple of answers. One is my ideal, perfect-world scenario, the Religious World According To Greta. The other is the world that, while not perfect, I'd be pretty happy with. The world where, if it somehow magically came into being, I'd quit writing about atheism almost entirely, and would turn my focus back to sex and politics and fashion and food.

So let's look at Greta's Perfect World first. In my perfect world, I would like to see religion disappear from the human mindset.

I think religion is a mistaken idea, and I think it's an idea that does more harm than good: if for no other reason, because it is a mistaken idea. I think it does harm, not just to atheists, but to believers. And I think it does harm even in the absence of overt religious intolerance. I think it disables reality checks. I think it encourages gullibility, vulnerability to bad ideas and charlatans. I think it discourages critical thinking and the valuing of evidence. I think it encourages people to prioritize wishful thinking over reality. I think the costs far outweigh the benefits, and I think the world would be a better place without it. Not a perfect place—I'm not deluded enough to think that the disappearance of religion would eradicate all social ills—but better.

So yes, I would like to see religion eventually disappear. I would not, however, like to see this disappearance happen in any sort of coerced or enforced way. I would not, for instance, like to see laws passed against religious beliefs or practices. I absolutely don't want violence done to people because of their religion. I don't even want social pressure exerted against religion or religious believers, except to the degree that arguments constitute social pressure. I want believers to be free to practice their beliefs however they choose, as long as that practice doesn't unreasonably impinge on my life or the lives of others.

That should all go without saying. But some people think that if atheists wants religion to end, we must want that end to come at the barrel of a gun. So I'm going to spell it out. I don't want religion ended by force. I want it ended by—insert barely-suppressed, self-deprecating guffaw here—persuasion.

No, really. I told you this was idealistic. So let's move on to the more scaled-back, more pragmatic vision. I would be perfectly happy to live in a world where:

Religious believers respected other believers and their right to their beliefs—including atheists and our right to not have any.

Religious believers understood that their beliefs were, in fact, beliefs and not facts, and didn't try to make laws and public policy based on them.

People, especially kids, understood that there were lots of different options when it came to religion—including the atheism option—and didn't have one version forced on them by intimidation or terror or the silencing of all other choices.

Religion didn't get the privileged, free-ride status it enjoys now, but instead was treated as just another hypothesis about the world, one which had to defend itself in the marketplace of ideas like any other.

If all that were true, I still wouldn't agree with religion. I'd still think it was mistaken. And I'd still probably debate it with people now and then. But I wouldn't be devoting my writing career to persuading people out of it. There are lots of mistaken ideas in the world. Urban legend debunking sites are full of them. I don't devote my life's work to their eventual disappearance.

But you wanna know the weird thing? I think my first vision, my vision of a world without religion, is more plausible than the second. I think a world without religion is a lot more likely than a world where religion is widespread but entirely tolerant and ecumenical.

Because tolerant and ecumenical religion is the exception, not the rule.

Daniel Dennett talks about this in his book, *Breaking the Spell: Religion as a Natural Phenomenon*. He argues that the essential baselessness of religion—the fact that it's unsupported by solid evidence or logic, that it's a shared opinion rather than a body of knowledge—actually makes people cling to it more tightly, defend it more vehemently, get more upset and angry when it's questioned. And the baselessness of religion makes people more likely to build elaborate defense mechanisms around it: from the tacit understanding that questioning religion is ill-mannered, to the harsh and even violent codification of religious beliefs into strictly-enforced law.

You don't need to build an entire cultural suit of armor around an obvious fact. If strange people came over the hill and insisted that the sky was orange, you probably wouldn't go to war with them about it. But people do go to war when strange people from over the hill insist that God is named Allah instead of Jesus, or vice versa. The idea that the sky is orange is easy to dismiss. You can see that it isn't. The idea that your whole concept of God might be mistaken… that's less easy to dismiss. And it's therefore, psychologically, much more important to defend.

When I look at the history of religion, and at religion in the world today, it becomes clear that the groovy, accepting, "we're all looking at the same god in our own way" style of progressive ecumenicalism is very much in the minority. Hostility to other beliefs—and super-hostility to no belief at all—is much more common. It's so common, in fact, that it seems to be one of religion's defining characteristics.

So yes, on a day-to-day political level, I'm going to fight for religious tolerance. Evangelizing out of the military, creationism out of the public schools, public health policy not being written by fundamentalists, that sort of thing. But I'm also going to keep fighting against religion. I'm going to keep working to keep atheism in the public eye, to make sure that every day, more people know about it and see it as a valid option. I'm going to keep persuading people out of religion, and keep building an atheist community that's a safe place to land when people leave it… so in a few generations, long after I'm dead, my ideal vision of a world without religion might someday be realized.

Because I think that's a much more attainable goal.

CHAPTER ELEVEN

— ❋ —

Is Atheist Activism Valid?

"Okay, sure. I understand why atheists are so angry about religion. But why do you have to try to convince everyone else to be an atheist? Isn't that what religious evangelists do? If you're trying to persuade people that atheism is correct, if you're working to change the world into one without religion—isn't that trying to create conformity? Why do you hate diversity? Aren't you trying to create a drab, uniform world, where everyone is just like you?"

It should be obvious that I think the answer is a big, fat "No!" But it's true that many atheist activists—myself among them—are working to persuade believers out of their beliefs. Not all atheists do this, of course; many have the more modest goals of religious tolerance and separation of church and state, including tolerance of atheists and recognition of us as equal citizens. But a good number of atheists are, in fact, trying to convince religious believers to become atheists. I'm one of them.

And since many believers see this as an intolerant attempt to enforce conformity—particularly believers of the progressive, ecumenical, "all religions perceive God in their own way and we have to respect them all" stripe—I want to take some time to explain it.

The Intolerant Bigotry of the Germ Theory

If there's a single idea I'd most like to get across to believers, it would not be, "There is no god." Or even, "There's probably no god." I want believers to reach that conclusion on their own. Upon being awestruck by my brilliant arguments, of course… but ultimately on their own, after thinking it through, after looking at the reasons for belief and the reasons for atheism, and finally concluding that atheism makes more sense. I don't want people to stop believing in God just because I say so.

If there's a single idea I'd most like to get across to believers, it would be this:

Religion is a hypothesis.

Religion is a hypothesis about how the world works, and why it is the way it is. Religion is the hypothesis that the world is the way it is, at least in part, because of supernatural beings or forces that act on the natural world.

Religion is many other things, of course. It's communities, cultural traditions, political ideologies, philosophies. But those things aren't what make religion unique. What makes religion unique, among all other communities and philosophies and so on, is this hypothesis of a supernatural world acting on the natural one. It's thousands of different hypotheses, actually, positing thousands of supernatural beings and forces, with thousands of different qualities and temperaments. But all these diverse beliefs have this one hypothesis in common: the hypothesis that there is a supernatural world, and that the natural world is the way it is because of it.

So religion is not a subjective opinion, or an ethical axiom, or a personal perspective. (These things can be connected with religion, of course, but they're not what make its unique core.) Opinions and axioms and personal perspectives can be debated—but ultimately, they're up to each person to decide for themselves. Religion is none of these things. Religion is a hypothesis. It says, "Things are the way they are because of the supernatural." Things are the way they are because God made them that way. Because the Devil is making them that way. Because the World-Soul is evolving that way. Because we have spiritual energy animating our consciousness. Because guardian angels are watching us. Because witches are casting spells. Because we're the reincarnated souls of dead people. Whatever.

Seeing religion as a hypothesis is important for a lot of reasons. But the reason that's most relevant here: If religion is a hypothesis, it is not hostile to diversity for atheists to oppose it.

It is no more hostile to diversity to oppose the religion hypothesis than it is to oppose the hypothesis that global warming is a hoax. The hypothesis that an unrestricted free market will cause the economy to flourish for everyone. The hypothesis that illness is caused by an imbalance in the four bodily humours. The hypothesis that the Sun orbits the Earth.

Arguing against hypotheses that aren't supported by good evidence... that's not anti-diversity. That's how we understand the world better. We understand the world by rigorously gathering and analyzing evidence... and by ruthlessly rejecting any hypothesis that the evidence doesn't support. Was it hostile to diversity for Pasteur to argue against the theory of spontaneous generation? For Georges Lemaitre to argue against the steady-state Universe? For Galileo to argue against geocentrism?

And if not—then why is it hostile to diversity for atheists to argue against the hypothesis of God and the supernatural? How is it any more anti-diversity for atheists to argue against religion, and to try to persuade believers that it's mistaken, than it is to argue a case against any other hypothesis?

Now. Many believers will argue that religion doesn't fall into these categories. They'll argue that religions can't be proven true or false... and that it's therefore reasonable for people to believe in any religion that appeals to them. (And that it's unreasonable for anyone to make an argument against it.)

But… well, for one thing, that's not strictly true. Many religions, from young-Earth creationism to astrology, *do* make testable claims. They *do* make claims that can be shown to be true or false. And every time those claims have been rigorously tested, they have always been shown to be false. They can't be disproven with 100% certainty… but almost nothing can, and that's not the standard of evidence we use for any other claim.

Much more to the point, though: When you start seeing religion as a hypothesis? The fact that it's unverifiable stops being a defense. It's completely the opposite. The fact that religion is unverifiable is one of the most devastating arguments against it.

A hypothesis has to be falsifiable. That's important. If any possible evidence could be used to support a hypothesis—if your hypothesis will be shown to be true whether the water in the beaker gets hotter, gets colder, stays the same temperature, boils away instantly, turns into a parrot and flies out the door—it's a useless hypothesis. If any event at all can be fitted into it, then it has no power to explain past events, or predict future outcomes. It is, as they say, not even wrong.

And that's just as true of religion as any other hypothesis. If any outcome of, for instance, an illness—recovering dramatically for no apparent reason, getting gradually better with medical intervention, getting worse, staying the same indefinitely, dying—could be explained as God's work… then the God hypothesis is useless. It has no power to explain the world, or to predict the future, or to tell us how our behavior will affect our lives. It serves no purpose.

The fact that religion is unfalsifiable doesn't mean we have to accept it as a reasonable possibility. It means the exact opposite. It means we should reject it wholesale, on that basis alone.

And it is not anti-diversity for atheists to point this out. Any more than it's anti-diversity to point out that any other hypothesis is unfalsifiable, or unsupported by evidence, or directly contradicted by evidence, or in any other way mistaken or flawed.

But You Hate Evangelism!

"But you hate religious evangelism! You hate it when religious believers scream into bullhorns and knock on doors to get people to come to Jesus! How can you argue against that, and then turn around and try to get people to come away from Jesus? How can you be such a hypocrite?"

Whenever I argue that it's okay for atheists to try to change people's minds about God, this argument almost always rears its head. And my answer almost always shocks the heck out of people:

I don't have a problem with religious evangelism.

Now that your jaw has stopped hitting the floor, let me explain. Of course I have problems with religious evangelism as it commonly plays out in the world. I'll get to that in a tic. But the very idea of religious evangelism? The idea that people who think they're right about their god should try to convince others about it? I don't have any problem with that at all. I support it 100%.

The problem with religious evangelism isn't that they're trying to change people's minds. Trying to change people's minds is a grand tradition. The marketplace of ideas, and all that. If you honestly think you're right about something important, of course you should try to share it. That's how good ideas get out in the world. And being exposed to different ideas is good for us. It exercises the brain. It's how good ideas get strengthened and clarified, and bad ideas get winnowed out. As Ursula Le Guin said in *The Dispossessed*, "The idea is like grass. It craves light, likes crowds, thrives on crossbreeding, grows better for being stepped on."

In fact, if believers were right, it would be monstrous of them *not* to try to convince others about it. For lots of religions, anyway. If there really was an eternal Heaven and Hell after we die, and this life really was just a temporary testing ground for it? It would be the moral obligation of every believer to devote every ounce of their time into converting as many people as they could. (The fact that most hard-line believers don't do this makes me suspicious of whether their beliefs are sincere.)

Now, all this acceptance of religious evangelism is largely in theory. In practice, I have serious problems with it. And I do think my attempts to persuade people out of religion are substantially different. For one thing: I'm not knocking on people's doors, or moving into their villages, or shouting at them through bullhorns on the street. I'm not invading people's lives or their privacy. I'm writing a blog, I'm giving talks, I'm writing this book. People are free to hear and read my ideas, or not, as they like. And outside the public sphere, I rarely offer my opinions on religion unless I'm asked.

But many atheists I admire do engage in more pro-active, in-your-face activism—putting up billboards, for instance, or going on TV—to spread the good word about God's non-existence. If the only difference between atheist activists and religious missionaries is that we don't knock on doors and shout at people on the street, I'm not sure that's enough difference to maintain my moral outrage at evangelism.

But that's not the only difference. The problem with religious evangelism, as opposed to atheist activism, is much bigger than the size and effectiveness of the bullhorn. The problem with religious evangelism isn't simply that they're trying to change people's minds.

The problem is with how they're doing it.

My efforts towards atheist persuasion are based in—here comes the broken record—reason and evidence. I offer arguments and reasons for why atheism makes more sense, is more consistent, is more likely to be accurate. And that's true of almost every atheist writer I know.

Religious evangelism does nothing of the kind. It bases its persuasion on fear: the normal fear of death, and the trumped-up fear of Hell and eternal torture. It bases its persuasion on false hope: a hope for immortality that the persuaders have no good reason to believe is true. It bases its persuasion on falsehoods: flat-out inaccuracies about the realities of history, and science, and even its own religious teachings.

And it bases its persuasion on the suppression of other ideas.

The suppression of dissenting ideas is one of the most widespread elements of religion. It's not universal, but it's depressingly common. It's codified in the texts and tenets of many religions: the concepts of the heathen and the heretic, the rules against interfaith marriage, the very notion of religious orthodoxy, and so on. It's often codified in law: not just in blatant theocracies, but in supposedly more enlightened societies as well. (It took until 1961 for atheists to be guaranteed the right to serve on juries, testify in court, or hold public office in every state in the United States.[1] That's the year I was born. It's not that long ago.)

And the silencing of dissenting ideas is codified in dozens of forms of social pressure. The idea, for example, that it's rude to question or criticize people's religion. The idea that religious faith automatically makes you a good person. The social deference given to ministers and rabbis and other religious leaders. The idea that being tolerant of religion requires that you not criticize it. Religion has built up an impressive array of armor: not intellectual weapons to defend its ideas, but armor to protect it against the very notion that its ideas require defending.

So yes to the marketplace of ideas. But in the marketplace of ideas, religion gets a free ride. In the marketplace of ideas, religion gets a free round-trip ride in a luxury limousine, with a police escort and an armored truck to transport its merchandise. All at public expense. And religious evangelism relies on that.

That's the difference. The problem with religious evangelism isn't that it tries to persuade other people that it's right. The problem is that it tries to persuade using fear, and false hope, and falsehood. And it tries to persuade by shutting up any other ideas that might contradict it. It tries to win, not by playing fair, but by rewriting the rules of the game.

A New Model for Diversity

I know that a lot of people will still have problems with atheist activism. Even if they know in their minds that atheist activism is fair and reasonable, they still have an instinctive reaction against it. For a lot of people, it seems like religious intolerance to say, out loud, in actual words, "Your religion is wrong, and I think you should change your mind about it."

And I think the problem comes from how we think of diversity.

Historically, we pretty much have two ways of dealing with religious beliefs that are different from ours. We have intolerant evangelism and theocracy—forcing religious beliefs down other people's throats, through social pressure at best, laws and even violence at worst. And we have uncritical ecumenicalism—the idea that all religions are at least a little bit true, that they're all part of a rich spiritual tapestry, that they're all perceiving one little piece of the truth about God… and that even if they're not, it's intolerant religious bigotry to criticize them or try to persuade people out of them. This second approach largely rose up in response to the old-school "intolerant theocracy" approach… so any criticism of religion automatically gets slotted into that ugly category.

Atheism is offering a third option. We're offering the option of respecting the freedom of religious belief… while retaining the right to criticize those beliefs, and to treat them exactly like we'd treat any idea we think is mistaken.

The atheist movement is passionate about the right to religious freedom. (With the notable exception of a few assholes on the Internet. Name me one movement that doesn't have its share of assholes on the Internet.) We fully support people's right to believe whatever they believe, and to practice whatever religion or non-religion they choose, as long as they keep it out of government and don't shove it down other people's throats. And we think this right is a foundation of human ethics, one of the most fundamental rights we have. We have no desire to overturn it.

Yet at the same time, we think the right to free thought and free expression includes the right to criticize other people's thoughts and expression. We passionately defend people's right to their beliefs... but we also defend our right to think their beliefs are silly, and to say so in the public square. We express our disagreement in a variety of ways— some more polite and respectful, some more insulting and mocking— but we damn sure think we have the right to express it.

And we see no reason to treat religion with any more deference than any other idea. We see religion as—yes, you guessed it—a hypothesis about the world. We see it as a hypothesis that has never once in all of human history been shown to be correct. We see it as a hypothesis—thousands of hypotheses, actually—that either have been falsified numerous times, or else, worse, are unfalsifiable and should be rejected on that basis alone. And we see no reason to treat it any differently from any other flawed, unsupported hypothesis. We see no reason not to criticize it, to ask hard questions about it, to make fun of it, to point out flaws in it, to point out the good evidence contradicting it, to point out the utter lack of good evidence supporting it... and to do our damndest to persuade people out of it.

Some people will be upset by this. Some people will be offended by this. Some people will even be insulted by this. People often get upset and offended and insulted when their deeply-held ideas and feelings are criticized, questioned, challenged, mocked, and refuted. And it's still reasonable, and fair, and even right, for people to do that. Daniel Dennett explained it perfectly: "I listen to all these complaints about rudeness and intemperateness, and the opinion that I come to is that there is no polite way of asking somebody: have you considered the possibility that your entire life has been devoted to a delusion? But that's a good question to ask. Of course we should ask that question and of course it's going to offend people. Tough."[2]

Most atheists could probably deal with a world that included religion, as long as it was tolerant of other beliefs and stayed the hell out of government. Some of us are skeptical about whether this is possible—see Chapter Ten, "What Do You Want, Anyway? One Atheist's Mission Statement"—but we'd be more or less okay with it. Many of us even enjoy some of the rituals and traditions of religion, as long as they don't involve actual religious belief. (Secular Judaism being the obvious example.) But yes, many atheist activists would like humanity to give up on religion. We think religion is a mistaken idea about the world. We think we can make a good case for that position. We think it's reasonable to try to persuade people that we're right.

And this is not an attack on diversity.

It is a defense of reality.

CHAPTER TWELVE

---✴---

Is Atheist Activism Effective?

"But what good will any of this do? Sure, religion is a bad idea. It's mistaken, and it does more harm than good. But you're never going to persuade anyone out of it. Believe me, I've tried. I've argued with people about religion—and it never works. Why do you waste your time?"

So far, much of this book has been aimed at religious believers, as much as it is at atheists. Of course I'm talking to atheists—I want to give atheists a voice, to put into words some things they may have been feeling and haven't been able to express. I want to give them something they can hand to believers who ask them, "Why are you so angry?" And I want to inspire them to take action. But I'm also talking to believers. I'm trying to explain why, exactly, so many atheists are so angry. I'm trying to explain why so many atheists feel so strongly about our anger that we feel compelled to speak out about it, and act on it. And I'm trying to explain why atheists are, you know, right: why we're right about our atheism, why we're right about our anger, why we're right to speak and act.

This chapter is different.

This chapter is aimed almost entirely at atheists.

A lot of atheists will read this book, and will nod vigorously throughout. "Yes, yes! Religion is awful! It screws up people's lives! It does way more harm than good! The very nature of it is inherently damaging! And besides, it's just not true—that's the key issue here, and that makes it harmful pretty much by definition! It's a terrible, hurtful, bad idea!"

But when it comes to trying to persuade people out of their beliefs, they give up in frustration. "It never works," they say. "Religious beliefs are too irrational, they're not held for intellectual reasons, they're held for emotional reasons—so there's no point in making rational or intellectual arguments against them." Or else they'll say, "Religious beliefs are too entrenched, people hold on to them too deeply, they'll never be persuaded out of them. It never works. Why should we waste our time trying?"

In a word: Bullshit.

It does work.

Ask any atheist writer with even a moderately sized readership. Ask me, ask Richard Dawkins, ask Jen McCreight, ask PZ Myers, ask any of us. We get emails *all the time* telling us, "I am now an atheist, in part, because of you." We get emails *all the time* telling us, "Your writings, your arguments against religion, are a big part of why I stopped believing." These are not isolated incidents. They're extremely common. It happens with atheists whose style is gentle and civil; it happens with atheists whose style is snarky and harsh. And of course, atheist writers have no way of knowing how many people we helped persuade out of religion... who never bothered to tell us about it.

If you're in any doubt about this—go to a local atheist meeting, or just go online to an atheist blog or discussion group. And ask people, "How many of you became non-believers—at least in part, not necessarily entirely, but in part—because of arguments against religion? How many of you had your minds changed, at least partly, by an atheist argument that you heard, or read, or saw on YouTube, or listened to in a podcast? How many of you had your deconversion process started, or moved forward, or had the final nail in the coffin driven in, by somebody's argument for why religion was mistaken and atheism was correct?"

I bet you'll be gobsmacked by the answer. The numbers are substantial. Most atheists used to be believers at one time… and many of us, maybe even most of us, were persuaded out of religion, at least in part, by arguments against it.

So why do so many people assume this never happens—to the point where they not only refuse to try, but work to persuade other atheists out of trying?

I think there are couple of reasons for this pessimism. The first is overly ambitious expectations. Yes, arguments against religion can—and do—persuade people out of their beliefs. But they rarely do so *right away*. I get lots of emails from people saying that my blog helped persuade them out of religion. But I've never argued someone out of their beliefs in the course of a single conversation. And I've never talked to an atheist who has. In fact, let's go back to your local atheist meeting or your online atheist forum, and ask for another show of hands. Ask people to speak up if they had their religious beliefs *partly* talked out of them by arguments against religion. And then, ask people to speak up if they were persuaded into atheism in the course of *one* conversation, by reading *one* atheist book, reading *one* atheist blog post, watching *one* atheist video, etc.

The first group is pretty big. The second—not so much.

A single argument is probably not, by itself, going to convince someone that their religion is mistaken. Religious beliefs *are* often deeply held. People usually *do* have them for emotional reasons as well as intellectual ones. Many people have never seriously questioned their religious beliefs, or even thought about them carefully. And letting go of them can be scary. It can be emotionally scary: you have to think about life, death, meaning, your place in the Universe, in radically different ways. And it can be scary in more practical ways. It can mean alienating your family, your friends, risking your job, maybe risking your safety. For most people, letting go of religion is a process. It takes time. And while other people can help with that process, ultimately it's something people need to do on their own.

So if you're expecting to persuade someone out of their beliefs in a single conversation, you're going to be disappointed. Don't let that discourage you. Don't think of it as winning or losing an argument. Think of it as helping someone along, helping them move a little further along their path. Think of it planting the seeds of doubt.

Or as nurturing seeds of doubt that are already there. This is a point that helps me be a lot more patient when I'm arguing with believers about religion. If someone is visiting an atheist blog or podcast or online forum, if they're attending a debate between an atheist and a believer, if they're visiting an atheist group and wanting to argue with you… chances are they're already having doubts. People don't visit atheist blogs or groups or debates or forums if they're not already a little curious about atheism. You probably won't demolish their faith in one dramatic explosion—but you may put another crack in the foundation.

I had a hard time grasping this concept in my early blogging days. I'd get into a debate with someone about their religion, and they'd seem reasonable and honestly willing to re-consider their beliefs, and I'd be positive that I could pry them out of those beliefs just with the power of my brain. I hadn't yet encountered the slippery excuses, the moving goalposts, the awesomely bad apologetics, the contorted logic, the flat-out denial of evidence, the flat-out denial of the idea that logic and evidence should matter when you're trying to decide what's true, the "I just feel it in my heart and that trumps any evidence you might show me" crap, the shifting of the debate from "Does God exist?" to "Why are atheists such jerks?" It was frustrating. To put it mildly. It's going to be frustrating to anyone who gets into these debates. And it got me wondering whether what I was doing had any point.

But then I started getting the emails, from people saying, "You helped me become an atheist." I started getting emails saying, "Your writings, your arguments against religion, are a big part of why I stopped believing." As my blog gets more widely read, I get more of these emails all the time. And it made me realize: Oh. This does work. It just doesn't always work right away.

So that's one reason many atheists are pessimistic about arguments against religion—they've never seen it work in the course of one argument, so they assume it never works at all. But I think there's another reason. I think many atheists convince themselves that arguing against religion is worthless because *they, personally, don't want to do it.* They don't like confrontation, they're afraid of alienating people, they want to avoid scenes.

And you know what? That's fine. If you, personally, don't want to argue people out of their religious beliefs, then don't. There are lots of ways to be an atheist; there are lots of ways to be an atheist activist; and we all have to go about it in our own way. If you choose to focus your arguments on things like anti-atheist bigotry or separation of church and state, instead of on whether religion is true? Or if you choose to not argue at all, about anything, if you choose to simply to be a positive model of happy, meaningful, ethical atheism? That is great. Knock yourself out. I am entirely sincere about that. That's all worth doing, and we need people to do that. If we're going to pry people out of religion, we need to give them a safe place to land when they fall—and I applaud people who are doing that.

But take responsibility for that choice. Don't say, "I don't argue about religion because it's always a waste of time." That's a cop-out. Say instead, "I don't argue about religion because I don't want to." As you start saying that instead, you may find yourself re-considering your choice—or you may not. But take responsibility for that choice. And don't get in the way of other people who are making the other choice. We are having an effect. What we're doing works.

• • •

Okay. That mini-harangue is over. Persuading people out of religion can work. So let's talk strategy. What, precisely, works? If persuading believers out of their beliefs isn't a waste of time... which arguments should we be making?

I've actually looked into this question. I've done a survey on my blog about which ideas convinced former believers to become atheists.[1] And here are some of the themes that cropped up.

The historical or scientific inaccuracy, internal inconsistency, lack of evidence, or just plain absurdity, of religious beliefs.

The immorality, unfairness, or other troubling aspects of religious beliefs.

The diversity of religious beliefs: different faiths with incompatible views, with no way to resolve those differences, and no reason to think one is more likely to be true.

The similarity of the Christian myth to other myths.

The lack of good evidence or arguments for religion, the failure of religion to make its case, and the bad arguments that get made for religion.

Seeing religion as rejecting intellect, reason, and reality.

Seeing science as a better explanation for X—consciousness, life, religious experiences, whatever—than religion.

Seeing that religion is more likely to be a human creation than a divine one.

Dishonest, hypocritical, or other bad behavior by religious believers or leaders.

Exposure to general skepticism, critical thinking, and the scientific method.

Exposure to specific scientific or historical ideas that contradict religion.

Simply knowing, or being exposed to, atheists or other non-believers; realizing that non-belief was an option.

Seeing that atheists not only exist, but can be happy people with moral, meaningful, non-guilt-ridden lives.

Realizing that "I only believed because it's what I was taught or what was expected of me."

Not getting good answers to questions about religion, or questions getting shot down.

Religion just seeming ridiculous, stupid, or pointless.

Seeing religion as based on logical fallacies or cognitive biases.

Seeing the harm done by religion.

Seeing the bad consequences of believing in absolute right and wrong.

Seeing bad things happening, which isn't consistent with a belief in a good god.

Seeing that morality is possible without God or religion.

Seeing religion as no different from other superstitions or gullible beliefs.

Not seeing religion as necessary.

Not seeing any reason to treat God as any more likely than any other implausible hypothesis: the invisible pink unicorn, Russell's teapot, the Flying Spaghetti Monster, etc.

The insufficiency of religion to offer comfort or other things it promises.

Realizing that they were cherry-picking: picking the tenets of their faith that they liked and rejecting the ones they didn't, purely on the basis of their own feelings, with no evidence about what God wanted.

Failed prophecies.

The factual and scientific impossibility, implausibility, and inconsistency of religious claims and texts.

Learning that Jesus might be a mythical figure, and that the historical Jesus might not be real.

Seeing religion as being just like other fraud or trickery.

Seeing how cognitive biases generate and support religion.

Seeing better evidence for evolution than creationism.

Seeing God as an unnecessary hypothesis.

Seeing that if one part of their religious text is inaccurate, there's no reason to believe any of it.

Seeing the internal inconsistency of their religion.

Seeing the inconsistency of their religion with human reality.

Seeing that atheism is potentially falsifiable, but most religions aren't.

Seeing how human behavior is like the behavior of other animals.

Seeing religion as no fun.

The "god of the gaps": the tendency of religion to say that any unexplained phenomenon must be explained by God, and the readiness of religion to jump to the next unexplained phenomenon when the previous one gets a natural, scientific explanation.

Realizing that religion didn't make people moral or special.

Realizing that "you don't choose your beliefs"—that beliefs need to be based on what you genuinely think is true and not what you want to be true.

Realizing that believers disbelieve in a lot of gods, too, and atheists just disbelieve in one more.

Realizing that intuition or feeling is not a good argument.

Realizing that the argument from popularity is a bad argument, and that the fact that lots of people believe something doesn't make it true.

Realizing that many religious apologetics are outright lies.

Seeing religion's unreasonable demands for unquestioning loyalty.

Seeing the importance of supporting your ideas with good, carefully gathered evidence.

Beginning to think independently in other ways, and questioning religion as part of that process.

Seeing religion mocked, blasphemed, made fun of, or made to seem silly.

Seeing terms such as "atheist" or "agnostic" accurately defined: realizing that it's possible to be both atheist and agnostic, and that atheism doesn't mean absolute certainty.

Leaving their church or other religious group, and realizing that their life got better or didn't get worse.

Encountering atheism or other non-belief and realizing, "Yes, that's me."

Emotional support from atheists.

And there are more that I don't have space to get into here.

All this may seem daunting. That's a lot of arguments to master. But the point is exactly the opposite. The point is that there's no magic bullet, no one argument that's going to convince everybody—so you get to make the arguments you know, the ones that resonate with you, the ones you're comfortable with.

So what's our game plan? If we're going to try to persuade religious believers out of religion—how, precisely, do we go about it?

Come out. This, by an order of magnitude, is the single most important thing atheists can do: to persuade others into atheism, or simply to create more acceptance of atheists. Often, just encountering atheists and atheist ideas can be a big factor in deconversion. And knowing about the existence of other atheists—especially other good, happy atheists—can help people feel like they have a safe place to land once they take that step. (The analogy with coming out as gay/lesbian/bi/trans is inevitable.)

Don't expect your arguments to deconvert anyone overnight. This rarely happens. So be patient. Don't think of yourself as dynamite under the foundations. Think of yourself as water wearing away the rock.

Don't expect to deconvert a strong true believer. Meeting atheists, encountering atheist ideas and arguments… these things can have an effect on believers. But they tend to have an effect in the end stage of deconversion—not at the beginning. The initial cracks of doubt typically come from within: from people considering their beliefs, and having doubts about whether those beliefs are moral, or consistent with reality, or even consistent with themselves. We can help widen those cracks… but we rarely make them happen in the first place.

That's not to say you shouldn't engage with strong true believers. The engagement can help strengthen your own arguments and clarify your own thinking. What's more, if the engagement is happening in any sort of public setting—an online discussion thread, say—it may have an effect on other people following the argument… even if they're not saying anything. And sometimes strong true believers *do* come around to atheism. Just don't count on it.

Remember that arguments can have an effect. I know how resistant to evidence religious belief can be. I know how frustrating it is to debate believers who don't seem to value reason. But lots of non-believers say that encountering atheists or atheist ideas was an important part of their deconversion process, and that they were at least partly persuaded by specific atheist arguments or ideas.

Again: We often come in at the tail end of the process, instead of at the beginning. But that's an important part. Don't dismiss it.

On the other hand, **no one argument is going to convince everybody**. We're not going to find a magic bullet, the One Good Atheist Argument that convinces everyone to deconvert. Different people find different arguments and ideas compelling. We have to keep presenting all of them.

Be willing to argue in public. Remember all those emails I get from people saying, "Your arguments helped persuade me out of religion"? There's a very important point about those emails: *They didn't come from the people I'd been debating*. They came from people who'd been lurking. They came from people who'd been following the arguments. It's possible that one of the people I tangled with is now a full-fledged atheist because of our debates… but if they are, none of them has told me about it. It's the onlookers who were persuaded.

So remember that. The people you're trying to convince? They aren't necessarily the people you're arguing with. They're the people who are looking on, who are following the comment thread or listening to the argument in the bar. This is true for big public debates, and it's true for little arguments on Facebook and in online forums and so on. So be willing to challenge the social convention. Ask questions about religion, contradict people about it, have debates about it… right out in the open, where other people can hear.

Expose people, not just to specific arguments against religion, but to methods of skeptical, critical, and scientific thinking. While specific arguments do help people deconvert, people generally need to begin the process on their own. But having critical thinking skills can help that process begin—and can help it come to its conclusion.

Encourage people to read the Bible or other sacred text of their religion. For lots of people, the loss of their belief started by examining more closely what they supposedly believed, and being either intellectually baffled or morally repulsed. (See Julia Sweeney's performance piece, "Letting Go of God,"[2] for a beautiful and hilarious example.) To put it more bluntly: For lots of people, the first step to losing their religion is reading the Bible or the Koran or what have you, and going, "It says WHAT now? Are you fucking kidding me?" Let's encourage more people to do that.

Build community. For many people—maybe even most people— the reasons they hang on to religion have nothing to do with theology. When you ask religious believers why they go to their church, synagogue, mosque, coven, etc., most say it's because of community. They want the social connection, the emotional support, the practical support, the feeling of belonging, the shared activities, the shared purpose. And when people start questioning their religious beliefs, letting go of all that is often one of the scariest parts. Letting go of religion often means alienating friends and family. Especially in parts of the world where religion dominates social life.

So atheists need to do more than just pry people out of religion. We need to give them a safe place to land when they fall. We need to develop secular and atheist communities, to replace the ones people often lose when they let go of their religion. (If you want to know where to look for these communities, see the Resource Guide at the end of this book.)

Finally, and most importantly:

Don't despair.

What we're doing can work. It is working.

What we're doing can feel frustrating to the point of futility. Religious belief is stubborn. It is resistant to reason and evidence. It is shielded with a wide variety of armors against criticism… and indeed, against the very idea that it can and should be subject to criticism. Trying to persuade people that their religious belief is a mistaken hypothesis about the world—even trying to get people to see their religious belief as a hypothesis at all, one which should be able to stand on its own against other hypotheses—can feel like shouting into the wind.

But what we're doing can work. It is working. Rates of non-belief have been going up dramatically in the United States and around the world, even in just the last few years. And in some parts of the world—specifically in Europe—non-belief is now so common that in some countries it's more common than belief.

And again—ask around in the local atheist group, the atheist blogs, the atheist online forums. Ask people why they're atheists, and what made them change their minds. And see how many people give a long, complex narrative… ending with the word, "Finally." "Finally I was persuaded by *The God Delusion*." "Finally I was persuaded by Daniel Dennett." "Finally I was persuaded by something my sister said, or my uncle, or my best friend." "Finally I was persuaded by something someone said on an internet discussion group." "Finally I was persuaded by something I read on this blog."

What we're doing can work. It is working.

So let's keep it up.

CHAPTER THIRTEEN

———✴———

On Other People's Behalf: Anger and Compassion

"But why are you atheists so angry?

"If atheism is so great—where does all this anger come from? Surely that's not a good sign. Surely it's a sign that you're dissatisfied, that you're self-absorbed, that you lack meaning and purpose in your life. Doesn't all this anger show that there's something wrong with atheists?"

Many people will read this book, and will agree with all or most of it. They'll read the first chapter, the long list of outrages committed by religion, and they'll be sickened and appalled. They'll agree that terrible, wicked, unthinkably hideous damage has been done, to millions of people, for centuries and indeed millennia, in the name of religion.

And they'll still think that atheists' anger proves there's something wrong with us. They'll think atheists are angry because we're selfish. Whiny. Absorbed in our own problems. They'll think atheists are angry because we're unhappy. Because we lack joy and meaning in our lives. Because we have a God-shaped hole in our hearts.

So I want to conclude by pointing out something about atheist anger.

Most of it isn't about how atheists are treated.

It's about how believers are treated.

Of course we're mad about damage done to atheists. And that's valid. There's real bigotry against us, real discrimination, and it's entirely fair for us to be angry about it. But most of our anger isn't about how religious believers treat atheists.

It's about how religious believers treat other believers. It's about believers getting taken advantage of by religious leaders. It's about believers getting AIDS because their church told them not to use condoms. It's about believers getting their genitals mutilated because their religion tells them their god demands it. It's about believers being terrorized into unquestioning obedience by the threat of eternal burning and torture.

It's anger on other people's behalf.

Atheists aren't angry because we're selfish, or joyless, or miserable. Atheists are angry because we have compassion. Atheists are angry because we have a sense of justice. Atheists are angry because we see millions of people being terribly harmed by religion, and our hearts go out to them, and we feel motivated to bloody well do something about it.

Atheists aren't angry because there's something wrong with us.

Atheists are angry because there's something right with us.

CHAPTER FOURTEEN

———— ✺ ————

What Now?

So now you're mad. (I hope so, anyway!) You're convinced that religion is not only mistaken, but inherently harmful. You're convinced that your anger is valid. You're convinced that acting on your anger is valid. And you're convinced that acting on your anger can be effective, and isn't a waste of time.

What can you do about it?

The next chapter has a list of resources for action. It includes activist organizations, local communities, print information, online information, online support, and lots more.

Pick one.

I, for one, would be happy for you to do any of this. Pick the ones that resonate with you. The ones you find inspiring. The ones you're good at. The ones you have time and resources for. The ones you think will be fun.

If you're angry about religion, and you want to picket the Mormon Church, or draw stick figures of Muhammad on your campus, or stick a nail through a communion wafer and throw it in the trash and post the pictures on the Internet… you should do that.

And if you're angry about religion, and you want to put up billboards saying that atheists are good people, or help organize fun social events at your local atheist meetup group, or simply come out as an atheist to your friends and family… then you should do that, too.

We need all of that. And all of that helps to dismantle religion.

Speaking out passionately against religion and its evils helps dismantle it. Persuading people that religion is mistaken helps dismantle it. Fighting against the unfair privileged status that religion enjoys in our society and our legal system helps dismantle it.

But making atheism more visible, and projecting a positive public image of atheism, and creating a fun, supportive atheist community… these also help dismantle religion. They refuse the social consent that religion relies on to perpetuate itself. They let people know that atheism is an option—and not only an option, but a valid and satisfying option, with joy and meaning. They give people a safe place to land when and if they leave their faith.

So if you're angry about religion, what should you do?

You should do whatever floats your boat.

You should do whatever form of activism you think is fun and inspiring. Wear an atheist T-shirt to the airport. Organize a same-sex kiss-in at the Mormon Church. Organize a canned food drive for your local food bank. Organize an atheist outing to a karaoke bar. Write a letter to the editor about anti-atheist bigotry in custody cases, or religious proselytizing in the military, or why you support the local atheist billboard campaign. Sponsor an atheist billboard campaign. Show up at your local atheist meetup group. Come up with ideas for activities for your local atheist meetup group… and help make them happen. Show up for the activities that your local atheist meetup group is already having. If there's no local atheist meetup group in your area—start one. Go to a show of an atheist musician, or artist, or slam poet. Link to nifty bits of internet atheism on Twitter or Facebook. Go to a school board meeting and insist that evolution be taught in science class. Go to an atheist conference. Organize an atheist conference. Organize an atheist film festival in your town. Host an atheist movie night in your living room.

Donate atheist books to prisons. Donate money to American Atheists or the Secular Student Alliance. Donate money to Camp Quest or the Foundation Beyond Belief. Start a blog. Put an atheist bumper sticker on your car. Get into arguments about religion on the internet. Tell someone you know that you're an atheist.

I'm happy with just about anything you might do.

As long as you do something.

CHAPTER FIFTEEN

Resources

This is by no means an exhaustive list. It's just meant to get you started.

ORGANIZATIONS

African Americans for Humanism
Supports skeptics, doubters, humanists, and atheists in the African American community, provides forums for communication and education, and facilitates coordinated action to achieve shared objectives.
aahumanism.net

American Atheists
The premier organization laboring for the civil liberties of atheists and the total, absolute separation of government and religion.
atheists.org

American Humanist Association
Advocating progressive values and equality for humanists, atheists, and freethinkers.
americanhumanist.org

Americans United for Separation of Church and State
A nonpartisan organization dedicated to preserving church-state separation to ensure religious freedom for all Americans.
au.org

Atheist Alliance International
A global federation of atheist and freethought groups and individuals, committed to educating its members and the public about atheism, secularism and related issues.
atheistalliance.org

Atheist Alliance of America
The umbrella organization of atheist groups and individuals around the world committed to promoting and defending reason and the atheist worldview.
atheistallianceamerica.org

Atheist Ireland
Building a rational, ethical and secular society free from superstition and supernaturalism.
atheist.ie

Black Atheists of America
Dedicated to bridging the gap between atheism and the black community.
blackatheistsofamerica.org

The Brights' Net
A bright is a person who has a naturalistic worldview. A bright's worldview is free of supernatural and mystical elements. The ethics and actions of a bright are based on a naturalistic worldview.
the-brights.net

Camp Quest

Residential summer camps for the children of atheists, freethinkers, secular humanists, and humanists.

campquest.org

Center for Inquiry

Their mission is to foster a secular society based on science, reason, freedom of inquiry, and humanist values. They have many local branches with regular meetings.

centerforinquiry.net

Church of the Flying Spaghetti Monster

A satirical church created to make fun of religion and point out the absurdity of teaching creationism in public schools. They hold that an invisible and undetectable Flying Spaghetti Monster created the universe after drinking heavily. Praise his Noodly Appendage!

venganza.org

Committee for Skeptical Inquiry

Their mission is to promote scientific inquiry, critical investigation, and the use of reason in examining controversial and extraordinary claims.

csicop.org

Council for Secular Humanism

Their mission is to advocate and defend a nonreligious lifestance rooted in science, naturalistic philosophy, and humanist ethics and to serve and support adherents of that lifestance.

secularhumanism.org

Council of Ex-Muslims of Britain

Non-believers, atheists, and ex-Muslims, are establishing or joining the Council of Ex-Muslims of Britain to insist that no one be pigeonholed as Muslims with culturally relative rights nor deemed to be represented by regressive Islamic organisations and "Muslim community leaders." *ex-muslim.org.uk*

Equal Rights Now—Organisation against Women's Discrimination in Iran

Established to promote women's freedom, emancipation and equality between women and men in the social, economic and political arenas as well as to strive for an end to sexual discrimination. *equalrightsnow-iran.com*

First Church of Liberty

Anti-faith based ministry for people on their quest to understanding life, the universe and everything. *churchofliberty.org*

Foundation Beyond Belief

A charitable foundation created to focus, encourage and demonstrate humanist generosity and compassion. *foundationbeyondbelief.org*

Freedom From Religion Foundation

Works to educate the public on matters relating to nontheism, and to promote the constitutional principle of separation between church and state. The Foundation is the nation's largest association of freethinkers (atheists, agnostics and skeptics) with over 17,000 members. *ffrf.org*

Freethought Kampala

A club that seeks to encourage dialogue between freethinkers in the Kampala area, and promote reason, logic, science and critical thinking in this highly superstitious society. *freethoughtkampala.wordpress.com*

The Freethought Society
Committed to education, investigation, and understanding.
ftsociety.org

Humanist Chaplaincy at Harvard
Dedicated to building, educating, and nurturing a diverse community of Humanists, atheists, agnostics, and the nonreligious at Harvard and beyond.
harvardhumanist.org

Humanist Community Project
This initiative, from the Humanist Chaplaincy at Harvard, is an attempt to research and provide resources to Humanist, skeptic, atheist and nonreligious communities around the country so they can build, grow and improve their local efforts.
humanistcommunityproject.org

Humanist Association of Ireland
Promote the ideals and values of Humanism: an ethical philosophy of life, based on a concern for humanity in general, and for human individuals in particular.
humanism.ie

Institute for Humanist Studies
A humanist think tank committed to information and practices meant to address the socio-political, economic and cultural challenges facing communities within the United States and within a global context.
humaniststudies.org

International Committee Against Stoning
Preventing the implementation of stoning sentences; fighting to abolish stoning.
stopstonningnow.com

The James Randi Educational Foundation

An educational resource on the paranormal, pseudoscientific, and the supernatural. Their mission is to promote critical thinking by reaching out to the public and media with reliable information about paranormal and supernatural ideas so widespread in our society today. *randi.org*

Kasese United Humanist Association

Promoting humanism and Free thought in communities around the country, with special reference to the Western Uganda region. *kaseseunitedhumanist.webs.com*

Military Association of Atheists and Freethinkers

Their mission is to provide a supportive community for nontheistic service members, to educate military leaders about nontheism, and to resolve insensitive practices that illegally promote religion or unethically discriminate against nontheism. *militaryatheists.org*

Military Religious Freedom Foundation

Dedicated to ensuring that all members of the United States Armed Forces fully receive the Constitutional guarantees of religious freedom to which they and all Americans are entitled by virtue of the Establishment Clause of the First Amendment. *militaryreligiousfreedom.org*

National Secular Society

Britain's only organisation working exclusively towards a secular society. Founded in 1866, they campaign from a non-religious perspective for the separation of religion and state and promote secularism as the best means to create a society in which people of all religions or none can live together fairly and cohesively. *secularism.org.uk*

Pakistani Atheists and Agnostics

PAA is about rational thought, compassion, science, freedom, and education. They provide a forum for freethinkers in Pakistan to get together, share ideas and strive for common ambitions.

e-paa.org

Recovering From Religion

If you are one of the many people who have determined that religion no longer has a place in their life, but are still dealing with the after-effects in some way or another, Recovering From Religion may be the right spot for you.

recoveringfromreligion.org

Richard Dawkins Foundation for Reason and Science

Their mission is to support scientific education, critical thinking and evidence-based understanding of the natural world in the quest to overcome religious fundamentalism, superstition, intolerance and suffering.

richarddawkinsfoundation.org

Secular Coalition for America

The national lobby representing the interests of atheists, humanists, agnostics, freethinkers and other nontheistic Americans.

secular.org

Secular Organizations for Sobriety

An alternative recovery method for those alcoholics or drug addicts who are uncomfortable with the spiritual content of widely available 12-Step programs. SOS takes a reasonable, secular approach to recovery and maintains that sobriety is a separate issue from religion or spirituality.

cfiwest.org/sos

Secular Student Alliance
Their mission is to organize, unite, educate, and serve students and student communities that promote the ideals of scientific and critical inquiry, democracy, secularism, and human-based ethics.
secularstudents.org

The Skeptic's Society
Their mission is to investigate and provide a sound scientific viewpoint on claims of the paranormal, pseudoscience, fringe groups, cults and claims between: science, pseudoscience, junk science, voodoo science, pathological science, bad science, non science and plain old nonsense. Publishes Skeptic Magazine.
skeptic.com

Society for Humanistic Judaism
Mobilizes people to celebrate Jewish identity and culture consistent with a humanistic philosophy of life.
shj.org

Stiefel Freethought Foundation
Provides financial support and volunteer strategy consulting to the Freethought Movement.
stiefelfreethoughtfoundation.org

United Coalition of Reason
A nonprofit national organization that helps local nontheistic groups work together to achieve higher visibility, gain more members, and have a greater impact in their local areas.
unitedcor.org

Women Against Fundamentalism
Challenges the rise of fundamentalism in all religions. Members include women from many backgrounds and from across the world.
womenagainstfundamentalism.org.uk

ONLINE FORUMS/RESOURCES/SUPPORT NETWORKS

Atheism Resource

Provides information about atheism from a historical, cultural, political, psychological, sociological, and scientific perspective.
atheismresource.com

Atheist Nexus

The world's largest coalition of nontheists and nontheist communities.
www.atheistnexus.org

Atheists of Color: A List

A list of prominent atheists of color, organizations of atheists of color, and atheist organizations predominantly focused on and/or participated in by people of color.
freethoughtblogs.com/greta/2011/03/21/atheists-of-color

The Clergy Project

A confidential online community for active and former clergy who do not hold supernatural beliefs.
clergyproject.org

ExChristian.net

Encouraging de-converting and former Christians.
exchristian.net

Free Inquiry

The magazine of the Council for Secular Humanism. Their mission is to promote and nurture the good life—life guided by reason and science, freed from the dogmas of god and state, inspired by compassion for fellow humans, and driven by the ideals of human freedom, happiness, and understanding.
secularhumanism.org/fi

The Freethinker
The voice of atheism since 1881.
freethinker.co.uk

Friendly Atheist Forums
Online discussion forum for readers of Friendly Atheist.
forum.friendlyatheist.com

God is Imaginary—50 Simple Proofs
It is easy to prove to yourself that God is imaginary. The evidence is all around you. Here are 50 simple proofs.
godisimaginary.com

Grief Beyond Belief
Faith-free support for non-religious people grieving the death of a loved one.
facebook.com/faithfreegriefsupport

Internet Infidels
A nonprofit educational organization dedicated to defending and promoting a naturalistic worldview on the Internet.
infidels.org

Iron Chariots
The counter-apologetics wiki. Collects common arguments and provides responses, information and resources to help counter the glut of misinformation and poor arguments which masquerade as evidence for religious claims.
ironchariots.org

A Large List of Awesome Female Atheists
A list of some great female atheists who you should check out if you haven't already done so.
freethoughtblogs.com/blaghag/2010/01/a-large-list-of-awesome-female-atheists

Lawyers' Secular Society

Provides advice and assistance to individuals affected by laws which give special advantages to those who assert religious beliefs. Based in Britain.

lawyerssecularsociety.org

RationalWiki

Refutation and analysis of anti-science and crank ideas; essays on right wing authoritarianism and religious fundamentalism.

rationalwiki.org

Secular Cafe

A place for mostly *secular* people to socialize, support, and discuss religion, science, politics, etc.

secularcafe.org

Skeptical Inquirer

The official journal of the Committee for Skeptical Inquiry. Publishes critical scientific evaluations of all manner of controversial and extraordinary claims, including but not limited to paranormal and fringe-science matters, and informed discussion of all relevant issues.

csicop.org/si

The Skeptics Annotated Bible/Koran/Book of Mormon

Passages of the Bible, Koran, and Book of Mormon are highlighted with a focus on their scientific inaccuracy, historical inaccuracy, contradictions, failed prophecies, absurdity, injustice, cruelty and violence, sexism, homophobia, and intolerance.

skepticsannotatedbible.com/

The Skeptic's Dictionary

Definitions, arguments, and essays on topics ranging from acupuncture to zombies, and provides a lively, commonsense trove of detailed information on things supernatural, paranormal, and pseudoscientific.

skepdic.com

South African Skeptics

An online skeptic community for and by South Africans.

skeptic.za.org

Truth Saves

It's time we all become more honest and knowledgeable about Christianity and its claims.

truth-saves.com

Talk Origins

A Usenet newsgroup devoted to the discussion and debate of biological and physical origins. Also provides articles and essays with mainstream scientific responses to those advocating intelligent design or other creationist pseudosciences.

talkorigins.org

Why Won't God Heal Amputees?

If you are an intelligent human being, and if you want to understand the true nature of God, you owe it to yourself to ask, "Why won't God heal amputees?" Start your exploration here.

whywontgodhealamputees.com

BLOGS/VIDEOBLOGS/PODCASTS

Greta Christina's Blog

Atheism. sex, politics, dreams, and whatever. Thinking out loud since 2005.

Yes, I'm putting myself first, out of alphabetical order. It's my book. Suck it up.

freethoughtblogs.com/greta

Freethought Blogs

The largest and most widely-read network of atheist, secular, freethought, and other godless bloggers.

And yes, I'm listing Freethought Blogs second, also out of alphabetical order, since they're the network I blog with.
freethoughtblogs.com

Al Stefanelli

A voice of reason in an unreasonable world. The blog of the Georgia State Director for American Atheists, Inc., and the author of *A Voice Of Reason In An Unreasonable World: The Rise Of Atheism On Planet Earth.*
freethoughtblogs.com/alstefanelli

Alethian Worldview

If it isn't reality, it isn't the truth. The blog of Deacon Duncan.
freethoughtblogs.com/alethianworldview

Almost Diamonds

Stephanie Zvan has been called a science blogger and a sex blogger, but if it means she has to choose just one thing to be or blog about, she's decided she's never going to grow up.
freethoughtblogs.com/almostdiamonds

The Anti-Intellect Blog

The inspired writing of a black gay rights activist, feminist, and atheist.
antiintellect.wordpress.com

An Apostate's Chapel

A former Protestant minister, now an atheist. This blog discusses her indoctrination into evangelical Christianity and her escape from that *worldview toward a more enlightened, rational position.*
thechapel.wordpress.com

AronRa

Video blogger. "I'm just doin' my part to raise awareness of science and the growing socio-political opposition to it."
youtube.com/user/aronra

Ask an Atheist

A call-in radio show featuring atheists from the Tacoma/Seattle Area. *askanatheist.tv*

Assassin Actual

The Internet is serious business. *freethoughtblogs.com/assassin*

Atheism: Proving The Negative

Analyses of God beliefs, atheism, religion, faith, miracles, evidence for religious claims, evil and God, arguments for and against God, atheism, agnosticism, the role of religion in society, and related issues. *atheismblog.blogspot.com*

Atheist Ethicist

A view of right and wrong, good and evil, in a universe without gods. *atheistethicist.blogspot.com*

The Atheist Experience

A weekly live call-in television show sponsored by the Atheist Community of Austin, geared at a non-atheist audience. TV show: *atheist-experience.com*, Blog: *freethoughtblogs.com/axp*

Atheist Media Blog

Your daily source of news & videos on science & religion. *atheistmedia.com*

Biodork

Thoughts from Brianne Bilyeu, a Minneapolis-based nerdy, liberal, humanist progressive, on topics such as science, skepticism, religion, atheism, critical thought, politics, and local and global humanitarian and equality efforts. *freethoughtblogs.com/biodork*

Black Skeptics

Spotlights the work of black skeptics, freethinkers, atheists, agnostics, humanists and other heretics who would dare to buck the orthodoxies of blind faith.

freethoughtblogs.com/blackskeptics

BlagHag

Profound thoughts from Jen McCreight, a liberal, geeky, nerdy, scientific, perverted feminist atheist.

freethoughtblogs.com/blaghag

Blasphemous Blogging

Blog of Edwin Kagin, National Legal Director for American Atheists.

freethoughtblogs.com/kagin

Blue Collar Atheist

Blog of Hank Fox, a happily godless author and blogger on atheism, religion and culture.

freethoughtblogs.com/bluecollaratheist

Butterflies and Wheels

Fighting fashionable nonsense. The blog of Ophelia Benson, columnist for *Free Inquiry* and the co-author of *The Dictionary of Fashionable Nonsense, Why Truth Matters, and Does God Hate Women?*

freethoughtblogs.com/butterfliesandwheels

Camels With Hammers

Daniel Fincke aims to discuss atheism, ethics, religion, Nietzsche, secularism, and general issues in philosophy in ways that are both accessible to non-philosophers and yet stimulating to professional philosophers.

freethoughtblogs.com/camelswithhammers

Canadian Atheist

A group blog of atheists from across Canada.

canadianatheist.com

Richard Carrier Blogs
Blog of the renowned author of *Sense and Goodness without God* and *Not the Impossible Faith*. He specializes in the modern philosophy of naturalism, the origins of Christianity, and the intellectual history of Greece and Rome, with particular expertise in ancient philosophy, science and technology.
freethoughtblogs.com/carrier

Comrade PhysioProffe
See for yourself.
freethoughtblogs.com/physioprof

Choice In Dying
Arguing for the right to die and against the religious obstruction of that right.
choiceindying.com

The Crommunist Manifesto
Blog of Crommunist, a scientist, musician, skeptic, and long-time observer of race and race issues. Bringing anti-racism into the fold of skeptic thought, and promoting critical thinking about even those topics that make us uncomfortable.
freethoughtblogs.com/crommunist

DarkMatter2525
YouTube channel. Humorous animations depicting the insanity of religion. Occasionally, they make a serious video.
youtube.com/user/DarkMatter2525

Daylight Atheism
Advocates secular humanism as a positive, uplifting and joyous worldview that deserves a larger following and wider recognition in the marketplace of ideas.
bigthink.com/blogs/daylight-atheism

The Digital Cuttlefish

The poet laureate of the atheist blogosphere.

freethoughtblogs.com/cuttlefish

Dispatches from the Culture Wars

Thoughts from Ed Brayton on the interface of science, religion, law, and politics.

freethoughtblogs.com/dispatches

En Tequila Es Verdad

Blog of Dana Hunter, a science blogger, SF writer, compleat geology addict, and Gnu Atheist.

freethoughtblogs.com/entequilaesverdad

EvolutionBlog

Commentary on the endless dispute between evolution and creation.

scienceblogs.com/evolutionblog

Friendly Atheist

I think of this as the Atheist Times. If you want to stay informed about current atheist news, this is the place to go.

patheos.com/blogs/friendlyatheist

Godless Bitches

This podcast was created to focus on feminist issues from a secular perspective and to help increase the presence of women's voices in the secular community.

godlessbitches.podbean.com

Happiness Through Humanism

Short posts about the Humanist philosophy designed to encourage people to live ethical lives of personal fulfillment that aspire to the greater good of humanity.

humanisthappiness.blogspot.com

Jesus and Mo
Religious satire from holy roomies Jesus & Mohammed in a twice weekly comic strip.
jesusandmo.net

Less Wrong
A community blog devoted to refining the art of human rationality.
lesswrong.com

Letters from a Broad
The adventures of a friendly American ex-Mormon atheist mom living in Switzerland.
lfab-uvm.blogspot.com

Living After Faith
A podcast called which addresses the process of coming out of religion, and how to live again after leaving the life of faith.
livingafterfaith.blogspot.com

Lousy Canuck
"Because I don't watch enough hockey, drink enough beer, or eat enough bacon." Blog of Jason Thibeault, an IT guy, skeptic, feminist, gamer and atheist.
freethoughtblogs.com/lousycanuck

Love Joy Feminism
Poking holes in piety, purity, and patriarchy. Blog of Libby Anne, an atheist, feminist, and progressive who grew up in a large evangelical homeschool family highly involved in the religious right.
freethoughtblogs.com/lovejoyfeminism

Mr. Deity
A webshow/podcast which looks at the everyday life of the creator and everything he must endure as he attempts to manage his creation.
mrdeity.com

Maryam Namazie
Nothing is sacred. Namazie is Spokesperson of the One Law for All Campaign against Sharia Law in Britain, the Council of Ex-Muslims of Britain, and Equal Rights Now—Organisation against Women's Discrimination in Iran.
freethoughtblogs.com/maryamnamazie

Taslima Nasrin
Physician, writer, feminist, human rights activist and secular humanist.
taslimanasrin.com

No Longer Quivering
Information regarding the deceptions and dangers of the Quiverfull philosophy and lifestyle.
nolongerquivering.com

No Religion Know Reason
Caribatheist's blog. Random reflections on atheism and faith from a born and bred West Indian.
caribatheist.blogspot.com

Non Stamp Collector
YouTube video channel. If atheism is a "religion"… then Not Collecting Stamps is a "hobby."
youtube.com/user/NonStampCollector

Pandaemonium
Blog of Kenan Malik, a writer, lecturer, broadcaster, author of *From Fatwa to Jihad: The Rushdie Affair and Its Aftermath*, a presenter of "Analysis," on BBC Radio 4, and a panelist on "The Moral Maze," also on Radio 4.
kenanmalik.wordpress.com

Pandagon
Progressive politics, feminism, atheism, other good stuff.
pandagon.net

Parents Beyond Belief
Thoughts and ideas by and for secular parents.
parentingbeyondbelief.com/parents

Pharyngula
Blog of PZ Myers. Evolution, development, and random biological ejaculations from a godless liberal.
freethoughtblogs.com/pharyngula

Qualia Soup
YouTube video channel. UK artist and secular humanist discussing critical thinking, science, philosophy & the natural world.
youtube.com/user/QualiaSoup

Reasonable Doubts
Your skeptical guide to religion. an award winning radio show and podcast for people who won't "just take things on faith." Its mission is to investigate the claims of religion from a fair-minded yet critical perspective. Blog and podcast.
freethoughtblogs.com/reasonabledoubts

Religion Dispatches
A daily online magazine that publishes a mix of expert opinion, in-depth reporting, and provocative updates from the intersection of religion, politics and culture.
religiondispatches.org

Rock Beyond Belief
Blog of foxhole atheist Justin Griffith, Military Director for American Atheists.
freethoughtblogs.com/rockbeyondbelief

Sincerely, Natalie Reed

Critical thinking on gender, sexuality, and other human matters. Reed was born with a Y chromosome but totally kicked its ass.
freethoughtblogs.com/nataliereed

Mano Singham

Thoughts on atheism, religion, science, politics, books, and other fun stuff, from a theoretical physicist and author of *God vs. Darwin: The War Between Evolution and Creationism in the Classroom*, *The Achievement Gap in US Education: Canaries in the Mine*, and *Quest for Truth: Scientific Progress and Religious Beliefs*.
freethoughtblogs.com/singham

Skepchick

A group of women (and one deserving guy) who write about science, skepticism, feminism, atheism, secularism, and pseudoscience. With intelligence, curiosity, and occasional snark, the group tackles diverse topics from astronomy to astrology, psychics to psychology.
skepchick.org

Spanish Inquisitor

Nobody expects the Spanish Inquisition!
spaninquis.wordpress.com

Susie Bright's Journal

Sex and politics. Stopped believing in "God" around 1968—a very big year for that sort of thing. "Could not be accused of shutting up."
—*Rolling Stone.*
susiebright.blogs.com

This Week in Christian Nationalism

Blog of Chris Rodda, author of *Liars For Jesus: The Religious Right's Alternate Version of American History*; Senior Research Director for

the Military Religious Freedom Foundation; and contributor to Talk2Action.org, Huffington Post.
freethoughtblogs.com/rodda

Thunderf00t
Video blogger. Science and Education FTW!
youtube.com/user/thunderf00t

Token Skeptic
Bending misconceptions with her mind. Blog of Kylie Sturgess, host of the Token Skeptic podcast.
freethoughtblogs.com/tokenskeptic

The Uncredible Hallq
Chris Hallquist has been an atheist blogger for over six years, which makes him like ninety in internet-years.
freethoughtblogs.com/hallq

What Would JT Do?
Fighting religion tooth and claw. Blog of JT Eberhard, co-founder of Skepticon, campus organizer and high school specialist with the Secular Student Alliance.
freethoughtblogs.com/wwjtd

Why Evolution Is True
Blog of Jerry A. Coyne, Professor in the Department of Ecology and Evolution at the University of Chicago, and author of *Why Evolution Is True*.
whyevolutionistrue.wordpress.com

The X Blog
Blog of Greg Laden, an anthropologist and science communicator who can never decide which is more important: nuance or context.
freethoughtblogs.com/xblog

The Zingularity
Blog of Steven Andrew, a struggling free lance writer and regular contributor to the popular progressive website Daily Kos.
freethoughtblogs.com/zingularity

ZOMGitsCriss, a.k.a. Cristina Rad
Video blogger. "I'm a shooting star leaping through the skies , I am a satellite, I'm out of control."
youtube.com/user/zomgitscriss

BOOKS

50 Reasons People Give for Believing in a God, by Guy P. Harrison

African American Humanism: An Anthology, by Norm R. Allen, editor

Amazing Conversions: Why Some Turn to Faith & Others Abandon Religion, by Bob Altemeyer and Bruce Hunsberger

Atheism: A Reader, by S.T. Joshi

Atheism: A Very Short Introduction, by Julian Baggini

Atheism: The Case Against God, by George H. Smith

The Atheist's Guide to Christmas, by Robin Harvie and Stephanie Myers, editors

Attack of the Theocrats!: How the Religious Right Harms Us All—and What We Can Do About It, by Sean Faircloth

Black and Not Baptist: Nonbelief and Freethought in the Black Community, by Donald Barbera

The Black Humanist Experience: An Alternative to Religion, by Norm R. Allen

Breaking the Spell: Religion as a Natural Phenomenon, by Daniel C. Dennett

Breaking Their Will: Shedding Light on Religious Child Maltreatment, by Janet Heimlich

By These Hands: A Documentary History of African American Humanism, by Anthony B. Pinn

The Caged Virgin: An Emancipation Proclamation for Women and Islam, by Ayaan Hirsi Ali

Confession of a Buddhist Atheist, by Stephen Batchelor

Darwin's Dangerous Idea: Evolution and the Meanings of Life, by Daniel C. Dennett

The Demon Haunted World: Science as a Candle in the Dark, by Carl Sagan

The Digital Cuttlefish: Omnibus, by Digital Cuttlefish

Does God Hate Women? by Ophelia Benson and Jeremy Stangroom

Doubt: A History: The Great Doubters and Their Legacy of Innovation from Socrates and Jesus to Thomas Jefferson and Emily Dickinson, by Jennifer Michael Hecht

The End of Biblical Studies, by Hector Avalos

The End of Faith: Religion, Terror, and the Future of Reason, by Sam Harris

Freethinkers: A History of American Secularism, by Susan Jacoby

From Fatwa to Jihad: The Rushdie Affair and Its Aftermath, by Kenan Malik

God: The Failed Hypothesis: How Science Shows That God Does Not Exist, by Victor J. Stenger

The God Debates, by John Shook

The God Delusion, by Richard Dawkins

God Is Not Great: How Religion Poisons Everything, by Christopher Hitchens

God vs. Darwin: The War between Evolution and Creationism in the Classroom, by Mano Singham

Godless: How an Evangelical Preacher Became One of America's Leading Atheists, by Dan Barker

God's Defenders: What They Believe and Why They Are Wrong, by S.T. Joshi

The Good Atheist: Living a Purpose-Filled Life Without God, by Dan Barker

The Good Book: A Humanist Bible, by A.C. Grayling

Good Without God: What a Billion Nonreligious People Do Believe, by Greg Epstein

The Gospel of the Flying Spaghetti Monster, by Bobby Henderson

The Greatest Show on Earth: The Evidence for Evolution, by Richard Dawkins

How We Believe: Science, Skepticism, and the Search for God, by Michael Shermer

I Sold My Soul on eBay: Viewing Faith through an Atheist's Eyes, by Hemant Mehta

In Defense of Atheism: The Case Against Christianity, Judaism and Islam, by Michel Onfray

Infidel, by Ayaan Hirsi Ali

Irreligion: A Mathematician Explains Why the Arguments for God Just Don't Add Up, by John Allen Paulos

Judaism for Everyone … Without Dogma, by Bernardo Sorj

Leaving the Fold: A Guide for Former Fundamentalists and Others Leaving Religion, by Marlene Winell

Letter to a Christian Nation, by Sam Harris

Liars For Jesus: The Religious Right's Alternate Version of American History, by Chris Rodda

Life, Sex and Ideas: The Good Life without God, by A.C. Grayling

The Little Book of Atheist Spirituality, by André Comte-Sponville

The Magic of Reality: How We Know What's Really True, by Richard Dawkins

Misquoting Jesus: The Story Behind Who Changed the Bible and Why, by Bart D. Ehrman

Moral Combat: Black Atheists, Gender Politics, and the Values Wars, by Sikivu Hutchinson

Nailed: Ten Christian Myths That Show Jesus Never Existed at All, by David Fitzgerald

Nomad: From Islam to America: A Personal Journey Through the Clash of Civilizations, by Ayaan Hirsi Ali

Not the Impossible Faith: Why Christianity Didn't Need a Miracle to Succeed, by Richard Carrier

Nothing: Something to Believe In, by Nica Lalli

The Only Prayer I'll Ever Pray: Let My People Go, by Donald R. Wright

Parenting Beyond Belief: On Raising Caring, Ethical Kids Without Religion, by Dale McGowan

The Portable Atheist: Essential Readings for the Nonbeliever, by Christopher Hitchens, editor

Quest for Truth: Scientific Progress and Religious Beliefs, by Mano Singham

The Quotable Atheist: Ammunition for Non-Believers, Political Junkies, Gadflies, and Those Generally Hell-Bound, by Jack Huberman

Raising Freethinkers: A Practical Guide for Parenting Beyond Belief, by Dale McGowan

Red Neck, Blue Collar, Atheist: Simple Thoughts About Reason, Gods and Faith, by Hank Fox

Sense and Goodness Without God: A Defense of Metaphysical Naturalism, by Richard Carrier

Sex & God: How Religion Distorts Sexuality, by Darrel W. Ray

The Skeptic's Dictionary: A Collection of Strange Beliefs, Amusing Deceptions, and Dangerous Delusions, by Robert Todd Carroll

The Skeptic's Guide to the Paranormal, by Lynne Kelly

Society without God: What the Least Religious Nations Can Tell Us About Contentment, by Phil Zuckerman

UFOs, Ghosts, and a Rising God: Debunking the Resurrection of Jesus, by Chris Hallquist

A Voice Of Reason In An Unreasonable World: The Rise Of Atheism On Planet Earth, by Al Stefanelli

The Ways of an Atheist, by Bernard Katz

What Do You Do With a Chocolate Jesus?: An Irreverent History of Christianity, by Thomas Quinn

Why Darwin Matters: The Case Against Intelligent Design, by Michael Shermer

Why Evolution Is True, by Jerry A. Coyne

Why I Am Not a Christian, by Bertrand Russell

Why I Am Not a Christian: Four Conclusive Reasons to Reject the Faith, by Richard Carrier

Why I am Not a Hindu, by Ramendra Nath

Why I Am Not a Muslim, by Ibn Warraq

Why People Believe Weird Things: Pseudoscience, Superstition, and Other Confusions of Our Time, by Michael Shermer

ACKNOWLEDGMENTS

First, last, and always: Ingrid.

I owe an enormous debt of gratitude to Susie Bright, for lighting a fire under me and getting me to freaking well write this book already.

The worst mistake Ingrid ever made was telling me she'd been an editor at her college newspaper. As a result, she consistently gets drafted into unpaid proofreading and copy editing duties. She read through several versions of this book, and helped on every level from tiny typos to the vision thing. I owe her more than I can ever say.

Thanks to my cover designer, Casimir Fornalski. You nailed it.

Thanks to Ophelia Benson, Susie Bright, Richard Carrier, JT Eberhard, Ben Gamble, Russell Glasser, Chris Hallquist, Greg Laden, Adam Lee, Alan Sokal, Al Stefanelli, and Stephanie Zvan, for reading early drafts of the book and pointing me in good directions. Any mistakes are all of my doing and none of theirs.

Thanks to Amy and Rob Siders at 52 Novels, for their excellent work on formatting.

Thanks to every single blogger in the Freethought Blogs network—and a special thanks to Ed Brayton and PZ Myers for creating it. I joined this network for professional advancement and to help advance our shared cause. I got a new family. It has been one of the best surprises of my life.

Thanks to AlterNet, and to my editors there, Tara Lohan and Tana Ganeva, for publishing my work and getting it read outside the atheosphere.

Thanks to my employers and colleagues Last Gasp, my day job, for their patience with my ever-shifting schedule, and for being an awesome bunch of brilliant and hilarious freaks.

I am enormously grateful to my blog readers. I get many of my best ideas from you. The Resource Guide was almost entirely crowd-sourced from you. And more to the point: You are the reason I do this.

And last, first, and always: Ingrid.

ENDNOTES

---✦---

CHAPTER ONE

[1] http://www.gallup.com/poll/26611/some-americans-reluctant-vote-mormon-72yearold-presidential-candidates.aspx

[2] http://volokh.com/posts/1125342962.shtml

[3] http://www.religioustolerance.org/texas1.htm

[4] http://www.militaryreligiousfreedom.org/

[5] http://www.thisamericanlife.org/radio-archives/episode/322/transcript

[6] http://www.bishop-accountability.org/news3/2007_09_20_StateofRhodeIslandandProvidencePlantations_DecisionOn_John_Petrocelli_1.htm

[7] http://www.commondreams.org/news2001/0917-03.htm

[8] http://news.bbc.co.uk/2/hi/south_asia/1222776.stm

[9] http://www.ushmm.org/wlc/en/article.php?ModuleId=10007058

[10] http://news.bbc.co.uk/2/hi/7926694.stm

[11] http://secular.org/issues/faith_healing

[12] http://secular.org/issues/childcare

[13] http://www.gallup.com/poll/145286/four-americans-believe-strict-creationism.aspx

[14] http://ncse.com/

[15] http://timesfreepress.com/news/2012/jan/04/christian-activist-questions-scope-of-anti

[16] http://freethoughtblogs.com/greta/2011/03/08/high-school-atheists-are-organizing-why-are-schools-pushing-back/

[17] http://freethoughtblogs.com/greta/2012/02/01/high-school-atheist-wins-unsurprising-court-case-gets-death-threats-why/

[18] http://freethoughtblogs.com/greta/2011/06/08/high-school-atheist-ostracized/

[19] http://www.nolo.com/legal-encyclopedia/recognition-same-sex-gay-marriage-32294.html

[20] http://mormonthink.com/lying.htm

[21] http://www.dailymail.co.uk/news/article-2093241/Mitt-Romneys-family-baptized-Ann-Romneys-atheist-father-Mormon-church-year-AFTER-death.html

[22] http://www.nytimes.com/2008/04/05/us/05jeffs.html

[23] http://www.deseretnews.com/article/595081003/Krakauer-still-vexed-by-FLDS.html

[24] http://qsaltlake.com/2010/11/11/homeless-gay-youth-in-utah-challenges-and-changes/

[25] http://freethoughtblogs.com/rockbeyondbelief/2011/11/06/suicidal-lesbian-marine-corps-vet-seeks-help-gets-jesus-instead/

26 http://www.theglobeandmail.com/news/world/worldview/in-jerusalem-women-are-voiceless-at-a-decidedly-womanly-event/article2297159/

27 http://www.msnbc.msn.com/id/27023066/ns/world_news-world_faith/t/jewish-modesty-patrols-sow-fear-israel/#.Tz6kUMqcOLI

28 http://www.washingtonpost.com/blogs/blogpost/post/naama-margolese-israeli-schoolgirl-says-she-was-bullied-and-spit-on-by-jewish-extremists/2011/12/27/gIQATNgRKP_blog.html

29 http://www.washingtonpost.com/blogs/blogpost/post/hillary-clinton-audrey-tomason-go-missing-in-situation-room-photo-in-der-tzitung-newspaper/2011/05/09/AFfJbVYG_blog.html

30 http://truth-saves.com/hitler-atheist-or-christian/ ; http://atheism.about.com/od/isatheismdangerous/a/HitlerAtheist.htm ; http://www.secularhumanism.org/library/fi/murphy_19_2.html; http://www.infidels.org/library/modern/mathew/arguments.html#hitler ; http://www.evilbible.com/hitler_was_christian.htm

31 http://www.huffingtonpost.com/2009/10/18/african-children-denounce_n_324943.html ; http://www.independent.co.uk/news/world/africa/witch-hunt-africas-hidden-war-on-women-1642907.html

32 http://www.guardian.co.uk/world/2009/mar/17/pope-africa-condoms-aids

33 http://www.usatoday.com/news/health/2010-01-26-1Ateenpregnancy26_ST_N.htm

34 http://www.guardian.co.uk/world/2009/may/20/child-abuse-catholic-schools-ireland

35 http://www.cbsnews.com/stories/2003/08/08/sunday/main567365.shtml

36 http://www.skepdic.com/exorcism.html

37 http://www.tv.com/shows/the-real-exorcist/

38 http://middleeast.about.com/od/religionsectarianism/a/me080923.
htm

39 http://www.nytimes.com/1993/07/03/world/40-killed-in-a-turk-
ish-hotel-set-afire-by-muslim-militants.html

40 http://www.africansuccess.org/visuFiche.php?id=461&lang=en

41 http://www.salon.com/2004/11/24/vangogh_2/

42 http://nolongerquivering.com/

43 http://www.tampabay.com/specials/2009/reports/project/ ;
http://exscientologykids.com/ ; http://www.newyorker.com/
reporting/2011/02/14/110214fa_fact_wright ; http://www.ameri-
camagazine.org/blog/entry.cfm?blog_id=2&entry_id=2193

44 http://www.infolanka.com/org/srilanka/cult/13.htm

45 href="http://www.breitbart.com/article.php?id=081128183857.
lgjbvt92

46 http://nihilobstat.info/2009/08/10/
the-dalai-lama-is-not-gay-friendly/

47 http://nihilobstat.info/2009/08/10/
the-dalai-lama-is-not-gay-friendly/

48 http://www.globalengage.org/issues/articles/freedom/590-buddhist-
nationalism-and-sri-lankas-christian-minority.html

49 http://freethoughtblogs.com/greta/2007/10/15/
atheists-and-an/#comments

CHAPTER TWO

1 http://freethoughtblogs.com/greta/2008/06/30/
the-screwed-up-teachings-of-jesus/

2 http://freethoughtblogs.com/greta/2007/08/15/eternal-fire-wh/

3 http://freethoughtblogs.com/greta/2007/10/15/
atheists-and-an/#comments

4 http://freethoughtblogs.com/greta/2009/02/16/shut-up-thats-why/

5 http://freethoughtblogs.com/greta/2008/06/30/
the-screwed-up-teachings-of-jesus/

6 http://freethoughtblogs.com/greta/2007/08/15/eternal-fire-wh/

CHAPTER FIVE

1 http://www.sfweekly.com/2004-09-29/news/friend-s-best-man/

2 http://freethoughtblogs.com/greta/2009/09/17/
how-dare-you-atheists-make-your-case/#comment-10270

CHAPTER SEVEN

1 http://www.tikkun.org/tikkundaily/2012/01/26/
reason-and-racism-in-the-new-atheist-movement/

CHAPTER EIGHT

1 http://skepticsannotatedbible.com/

2 http://skepticsannotatedbible.com/

3 http://freethoughtblogs.com/greta/2010/05/11/why-the-universe-is-
perfectly-set-up-for-life-is-a-terrible-argument-for-god/

[4] http://freethoughtblogs.com/greta/2010/05/04/argument-from-design/

[5] http://www.ebonmusings.org/atheism/burningbush.html

[6] http://answers.google.com/answers/threadview?id=272042

[7] http://andrewgelman.com/2009/06/future_trends_f_1/

[8] http://freethoughtblogs.com/greta/2008/09/07/in-defense-of-atheist-blogging/#comment-13786

[9] http://www.youtube.com/watch?v=w0ffwDYo00Q

CHAPTER NINE

[1] Phil Zuckerman, *Society without God: What the Least Religious Nations Can Tell Us About Contentment* (New York: NYU Press, 2010).

[2] http://freethoughtblogs.com/bluecollaratheist

[3] http://www.daylightatheism.org/2007/10/on-atheist-janitors.html

CHAPTER TEN

[1] http://www.religioustolerance.org/texas1.htm

[2] http://www.takeonit.com/expert/222.aspx

CHAPTER TWELVE

[1] http://freethoughtblogs.com/greta/2011/11/10/what-convinced-you-a-survey-for-non-believers/

[2] http://www.juliasweeney.com/letting_go_mini/

ABOUT GRETA CHRISTINA

Greta Christina is one of the most widely-read and well-respected bloggers in the atheist blogosphere. She blogs at the cleverly named Greta Christina's Blog, and is a regular contributor to the online political magazine, AlterNet. She was ranked by an independent analyst as one of the Top Ten most popular atheist bloggers, and her writing has appeared in numerous magazines, newspapers, and anthologies, including *Ms.*, *Penthouse*, *Skeptical Inquirer*, the *Chicago Sun-Times*, and the anthology *Everything You Know About God Is Wrong*. She is editor of the Best Erotic Comics anthology series and of *Paying For It: A Guide by Sex Workers for Their Clients*, and is author of *Bending*, an erotic novella in the three-novella collection *Three Kinds of Asking For It*. She has been writing professionally since 1989, on topics including atheism, skepticism, sexuality and sex-positivity, LGBT issues, politics, culture, and whatever crosses her mind. She is on the speakers' bureaus of the Secular Student Alliance and the Center for Inquiry. She tweets at @ GretaChristina. She lives in San Francisco with her wife, Ingrid.

Other Recent Titles from Pitchstone

Attack of the Theocrats!
How the Religious Right Harms Us All
—and What We Can Do About It
by Sean Faircloth

Candidate Without a Prayer:
An Autobiography of a Jewish Atheist in the Bible Belt
by Herb Silverman

PsychoBible:
Behavior, Religion & the Holy Book
by Armando Favazza, MD

Why We Believe in God(s):
A Concise Guide to the Science of Faith
by J. Anderson Thomson, Jr., MD, with Clare Aukofer